Tunnel books, covered in Chapter 8, are little dioramas, or stage sets, with each strip of scenery formed by a page between concertinas. Alice Simpson (United States), *Miss Brunswick Diner,* 1995. Paper, gouache with wooden stools by Alan Bradstreet, poetry by the artist, 8 x 16 x 10" (20 x 40 x 25 cm).

HANDMADE BOOKS AND CARDS

JEAN G. KROPPER

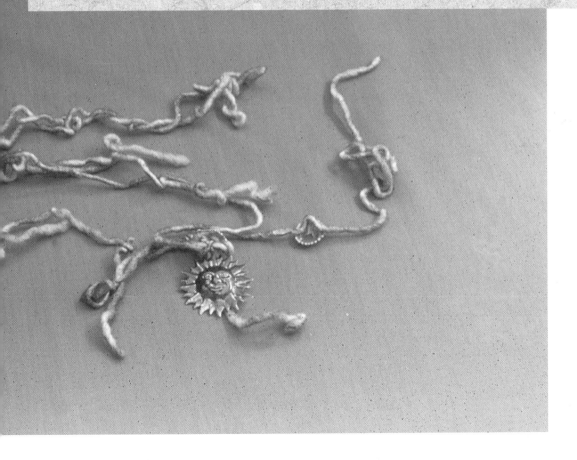

DAVIS PUBLICATIONS, INC. WORCESTER, MASSACHUSETTS

Publisher: Wyatt Wade
Editorial Director: Helen Ronan
Production Editors: Nancy Wood Bedau, Nancy Burnett
Manufacturing Coordinator: Steven Vogelsang
Copyeditors: Thomasine Berg, Lynn Simon
Design: Douglass Scott, Tong-Mei Chan
Illustrations: Jean G. Kropper
Assistant Production Editor: Carol Harley
Editorial Assistance: Jane DeVore, Colleen Fitzpatrick, Robin Banas

Library of Congress Catalog Card Number: 97–065423

ISBN: 0-87192-334-3

10 9 8 7 6 5 4 3 2 1

Printed in the United States on recycled paper

Cover:
Inga Hunter (Australia), *Imperium Scroll*, 1994.
5 1/8" x 3' 5/16" (13 cm x 1 m). (See page 124 for additional details.)

Front cover:
Top: Nancy La Rose, (United States), *Handmade Greeting Cards*, 1995. Hand marbled, hand combed papers, ribbons, hand-dyed silk, metal, and natural materials. 6 x 4 1/2" (15.2 x 11.4 cm).
Bottom: Jean G. Kropper (Australia), *Journal for a Sea Voyage* (left) and *Journal for a Wandering Mind* (right). (See page 56 for details.)

Back cover:
Lynne Perrella (United States), *Articulation for Frida*, 1995. Photocopies, rubber stamps, ribbon, and various papers, 17 x 10" (42.5 x 25 cm).

Title Page:
Jean G. Kropper (Australia), *Out of Prehistory*, 1995. Various plant fiber and recycled papers handmade by the artist (some embossed), wool, stones, and beads, 11 7/8 x 23 5/8" (42.5 x 25 cm).

Above:
Jean G. Kropper (Australia), *Autumn Leaves Book*, 1995. Concertina book with pockets, recycled paper. Machine embroidery and fabric paint, 5 x 3" (12.5 x 7.5 cm).

DEDICATION
For Nancy Gray, with love and thanks.

ACKNOWLEDGMENTS

I would like to thank Adèle Outteridge (Brisbane) and Alison Steele (Sydney) in Australia, my first bookbinding teachers. Adèle's creative ideas fired my imagination and got me started in bookbinding. Alison's technical advice gave me the skills to carry out my own projects and ideas. Daphne Dobbyn (Sydney) later added a great deal to my technical bookbinding education. Robin Tait (Queanbeyan, ACT, Australia) and Eric Hanson (Sydney) gave generous help on bookbinding questions. Peter Thomas (California) helped by sharing his thoughts on fine print books and Betz Salmont by teaching me to make star cards.

Photography by Eardley Lancaster (Sydney) and calligraphy on some of my cards and books by Olive Bull (Holland Park, QLD, Australia) is much appreciated. Their professionalism and good humor made a big difference. Thanks to Pierpont Morgan Library, the Spencer Collection at the New York Public Library, the Center for Book Arts in New York City, and Harvard University's Houghton Library, which helped with photographs on a tight deadline. The high quality of the rest of the photographs is due to the 160 artists worldwide who submitted over 900 images, and those who helped me by telling others about this project. All my students in the United States, Canada, and Australia have also helped, by teaching me as I taught them.

Lastly, thanks to my mother, Nancy Gray, of Fort Collins, Colorado, and to my husband and partner, Andrew Buist, of Denistone East (Sydney), Australia, for their help and support from beginning to end.

CONTENTS

Betz Salmont (United States), *Flag Book*, 1995. Handmade and commercial papers, 4 1/4 x 3/4 x 5 1/4" (10.8 x 1.9 x 13.3 cm), when closed.

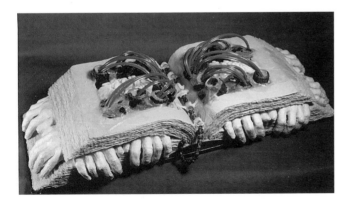

Dianne L. Reeves (United States), *Enlightened Prodigality*, 1993. Handmade paper from Abaca and Maguey fibers (from the agave or century plant, Mexico), plaster, seedpods, bones, tubing, PVA and silicon glues, 8 x 32 x 13 1/2" (20.3 x 81.3 x 34.3 cm).

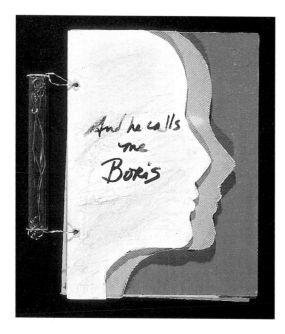

Karen Klein (United States), *Federman,* 1991. Book board, acetate, acrylic, mesh, feathers, ink, 5 1/2 x 7 1/4" (14 x 18.4 cm).

Deborah Papathanasiou (United States), 1995. Collage card with watercolor paper and stamping, 5 x 7" (12.7 x 17.8 cm).

Adèle Outteridge (Australia), *Brown Paper Book,* 1989. Used brown paper sewn on tapes, and bound in hard covers with handles, 9 5/8 x 6 1/2 x 2" (24.5 x 16.5 x 5 cm), when closed.

PREFACE

"What can I make with my papers?" my students asked at the end of my hand-papermaking workshops. As I heard this question again and again, I had many ideas for a comprehensive answer. Gradually, I started writing, and the ideas became this book.

You do not need to be an artist to create something both beautiful and useful. Making cards or books, or decorating papers, is a process. If you follow the steps of the process, learning skills along the way, you will get a result. With practice, you will make cards and books that please you. Although creative ideas may come more readily to artists, they too need to learn the steps of the process.

Since the 1970s, when the ancient art of hand-bookbinding (along with paper-making and calligraphy) experienced a revival, it has grown both as a technical craft and as a creative art form, two ends of the spectrum in bookbinding. However, there is a gap between these two that I would like to fill.

A beginner may take a class to learn how to make a particular binding, and yet not be given an understanding of how that binding functions and how to design for it. On the other hand, artistic approaches to bindings might focus solely on the artist's message or concept without presenting the practical concerns for binding a book that will endure. This book closes the gap by helping the binder design books that communicate in richer, more personal, and expressive ways; and by helping the artist gain practical skills in binding.

A hand-bound book—one with exotic and handmade papers and pages of different colors; one with an unusual shape; one that is large or small, square or round—offers design possibilities not feasible for commercial books. All these choices help the creator of handmade books express his or her message.

Coptic book. Adèle Outteridge (Australia), *Heart Book for Inga*, 1995. Handmade paper, acrylic paint, 2 3/4 x 2" (7 x 5 cm) closed; 4" wide (10 cm) open.

Along with books, cards are a means of communication. Books tell stories; greeting cards express sentiments and acknowledge special events in our lives: births, birthdays, weddings, promotions, and holidays. Making your own cards may not only save you money, but may also add a unique personal touch to your good wishes.

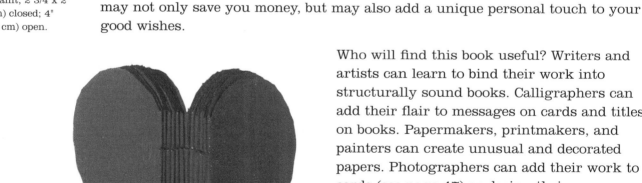

Who will find this book useful? Writers and artists can learn to bind their work into structurally sound books. Calligraphers can add their flair to messages on cards and titles on books. Papermakers, printmakers, and painters can create unusual and decorated papers. Photographers can add their work to cards (see page 47) or design their own albums. Traditional craft bookbinders can use creative suggestions to personalize their books. These specialists—and anyone else who loves working with paper—can use, and enjoy, the process of making handmade books and cards.

Pop-up concertina book. Nancy Callaghan (United States), *Pop-Pull-Spin,* 1995. Embossed, punched, pierced, woven, and cut papers, 5 x 6 x 2 1/2" (12.7 x 15.2 x 6.35 cm) when closed.

For the student, bookbinding offers cross-disciplinary applications. A literature student might write stories or poetry and then bind the works. A theater student might design a stage set and then try it out as a tunnel book. A history student might take on the role of undercover spy and write a secret message to be smuggled out of enemy territory. A political science student might express his or her views on international events in an altered book, or with a book whose text is a collage of newspaper headlines. An art student might experiment with the book as a sculptural form. Any student might bind a written paper, with its accompanying illustrations and photographs, to create a unique book as a finished package. The process of putting a book together forces its maker to organize, clarify, and sequence thoughts—skills useful in any field.

With the increased use of faxes, e-mail, and the Internet, the personal quality of communication is sacrificed to speed and convenience. Ironically, handmade cards and books take on new meaning because of their tangible, tactile quality and the obvious touch of their maker. When I receive a handmade card from a friend, I recognize the handwriting, see the person's choice of colors, the texture of the paper, the foreign postage stamp, and the local cancellation mark. I know the letter has journeyed from his or her hands to mine.

My goal is to introduce more people to bookbinding and cardmaking, to make their creation achievable, and to expand their application by combining the basic technical skills and creative ideas. All the books and cards described in this book can be made in one day or less and require few specialized tools. There are many variations to the bindings presented here; I offer my version.

The materials, messages, techniques, and goals of the works submitted for this book from artists around the world vary tremendously. Upon receiving the photographs of the works, I was awed, delighted, and humbled. I hope to pass that on to you with this book.

Jean G. Kropper
Sydney, Australia

LEARNING FROM MISTAKES

Often, you learn by experimenting to see if something works. If what you tried did *not* work, you can sit back and try to figure out what you could do differently so that it *will* work. That is, you look at the mistake and learn from it. Mistakes are tools for learning. Remember, most creative advances come from asking, "I wonder what would happen if I tried that?"

BUT I'M NOT AN ARTIST

Although some people have a gift for design, you do not need to be an artist or have any training or art background to be able to create books and cards. There is nothing magical about binding a book or making a card; both the artist and the nonartist have to go through the sometimes awkward steps of learning a process and techniques. What you do need to do is follow the steps, practice, and learn from mistakes.

USES FOR HAND-BOUND BOOKS

What are the uses for hand-bound books? Recipes, poetry, price lists, or even phone messages may be entered into the blank pages of a Japanese stab-bound book. Letters from a trip overseas, a postcard collection, theater programs, old love letters, or cards received for an eighteenth birthday or the birth of a new baby may be stored in concertina books. Memorabilia from a vacation, a series of sketches or watercolors, newspaper clippings, wedding photos, or comments from visitors at a guest house may be preserved in a hardcover album; and class notes or a collection of magazines or newsletters may be bound in a Coptic binding.

Once you determine what kind of book you need (see Chapter 6), you can then design and bind your own book. When you buy a ready-made commercial book, all the creative choices have been made. When you bind your own book, you make the choices.

IF YOU ARE THE TEACHER

Students learn in different ways: some by listening to instructions (auditory); some by seeing things demonstrated, drawn, or written down (visual); some by doing a technique themselves (kinesthetic). Many of us learn through a combination of these learning styles; others through only one. You do not need to figure out whether an individual student is an auditory, visual, or kinesthetic learner, although you may want to know this. What is important is understanding learning differences so that you can teach in ways that are more likely to reach all of your students. (See Resources, page 145.)

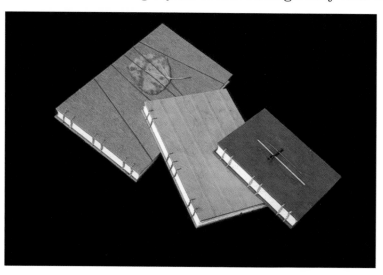

The covers and endpapers of these Coptic-stitched books feature papers handmade from plant fibers from the Philippines, Japan, and Thailand. Blank pages, made from acid-free paper, are ideal for poetry, prose, sketching, or calligraphy. Tracy Rittenberry (United States), 1995. Decorative papers, bound with waxed linen thread. Back to front: 10 x 5 3/4" (25.4 x 14.6 cm); 7 1/4 x 5 1/4" (18.4 x 13.3 cm); 5 1/4 x 4" (13.3 x 10.2 cm).

Freedom is not an abstract concept to the artist, who fled Czechoslovakia in 1968, during the communist invasion, to find safety in Canada. Included inside is the poem inscribed on the pedestal of the Statue of Liberty. Dana Velan (Canada), *Freedom Book,* 1993. Scrapbook with painting, a collage of postcard images, photography, and writing in gold pen; single-section pamphlet book on black Arches paper folios, bound with leather thongs with beads, 15 x 15" (38.1 x 38.1 cm).

PRACTICAL SOLUTIONS FOR THE TEACHER

To explain the steps of each technique or binding, I create simple, word-processed handouts on colored papers or place hand-drawn posters around the room (or I have students use this book). At the beginning of a class or workshop, I explain in general terms what we will cover. Next a student reads aloud a paragraph or two from the handout (book or poster), or with young students I read the information aloud myself. For further understanding, I paraphrase what was read, then check to see if the class has understood. Throughout this book, when appropriate, I have suggested alternative, simpler steps for young students.

Visual students can *see* the information on the handout, poster, or book and keep it at hand for review. Auditory students can *hear* the information from oral readings. Kinesthetic students can be active in a way that supports their learning by becoming familiar with tools and supplies by helping to distribute them to other students, and by doing the projects themselves.

At the end of a class or workshop, I have students read the same information again, often in pairs or small groups. Kinesthetic learners may instead choose to demonstrate (or mime) steps to their classmates. The students are instructed to check that they understand all the information and, if not, to answer one another's questions within the group. The students teach one another and hear explanations in each other's words; they may ask me only what no one in their group knows. These techniques help the students understand more information in the time available.

1–1 Cuneiform characters, the alphabet of Babylon and other ancient civilizations, record the details of a court trial that occurred over 3,000 years ago. The object on the left served as an envelope for storage. *Tablet and envelope*, c. 1500–1400 BC, clay. Tablet is 7 x 3 3/4 x 1 1/2" (17.8 x 9.3 x 3.8 cm); envelope is 7 1/4 x 4 3/4 x 2 1/4" (18.5 x 11.7 x 5.6 cm). Oriental Institute Museum, University of Chicago.

1–2 This piece mimics one of the earliest forms of storing written information, long before the invention of books. Clay tablets were made as early as 4000 BC in Mesopotamia. Ans Jacobs-Schotel (Netherlands), *Clay Tablet II,* 1995. Handmade recycled paper with pastel crayon, 7 3/4 x 7 3/4" (20 x 20 cm).

HISTORY OF BOOKS AND CARDS

Thirty thousand years ago, with drawings on cave walls, people began to record events, write down stories, and keep accounts. These drawings progressed to carved stone runes in Scandinavia, clay tablets in Sumer (part of ancient Babylonia), sheets and scrolls of papyrus, pamphlet books of parchment, and today's multisection books of paper. The history of books has been linked to available materials, the politics of competing libraries, and the known methods of reproduction and binding techniques. Each culture developed its own methods, and thereby contributed to the varied book forms we use now.

THE BOOK FORM

Book forms sometimes developed concurrently in different parts of the world. Often, both new and old book forms or writing materials were in use at the same time and place, as people had to become used to what was new before dropping old ways.

PAPYRUS SCROLLS

Around 3500 BC, Egyptians developed the writing system of hieroglyphics, and by 2700 BC, the process of making sheets of writing material from the papyrus plant. The plant was sliced into strips, stacked in layers, and then put under pressure, which fused the layers. Because the papyrus was too brittle to fold, it was rolled into scrolls for storage. Papyrus scrolls were adopted by the Greeks about 500 BC and by the Romans by 300 BC, and they were used by the Egyptians until the 900s.

BAMBOO AND PALM FRONDS

The earliest Chinese books were made about 3,000 years ago from bamboo or wood strips tied together. By the end of the fourth century, in India and Southeast Asia, books were written on the back of palm leaves two or three inches wide (5–7.5 cm) and twenty-four inches long (60 cm). Sometimes, these were fastened together with strings and opened like fans or unfurled like blinds.

1–3a, b The sections of this blind format book are incised with images that tell a sequential story. To close, the sections slide together, and the cord is wrapped around them. *Palm Leaf Book from Indonesia,* 1980s. Each section is 9 1/2 x 1 1/2" (240 x 38 mm). Courtesy of Daphne Dobbyn, Australia.

★ WOODEN TABLETS

The origin of wooden tablets, several hundred years BC, is unclear. Early versions were usually a thin wooden board with writing scratched into a polished surface. Later, the surface was painted with white gesso and black wax, and scratched with a stylus. Boards could be reused by smoothing out the wax. A raised edge around the "page" prevented the wax from being flattened. Tablets were common for everyday use by the Greeks and Romans; papyrus scrolls were used for more important documents.

❋ THE CODEX

Around 300 AD, the Romans drilled holes into the sides of wooden tablets and linked them together with cords or leather thongs. They called this a *codex*, from the Latin word *caudex*, meaning "tree trunk." Later, papyrus—and then parchment—replaced the wooden boards, and *pages* were stitched together.

Early book forms

| codex of wooden tablets | scroll | concertina |

🌲 PAPER

The Chinese had no papyrus, but they developed their own material for writing. They experimented with scrolls of silk fabric, but found it expensive. By 105 AD, they were making paper from hemp rope, old fishing nets, silk, and cotton rags. To form sheets of paper, a major improvement over papyrus, pulp was molded on a screen floating in water. Realizing the importance of their discovery, the Chinese kept the process secret for hundreds of years.

🦅 THE CONCERTINA BOOK

Because paper could be folded, the Chinese developed the *concertina* by folding a long strip of paper, instead of rolling it into a scroll. Referring to any one *section* of a text was accomplished simply by flipping pages. Use of this *format*, also called an *accordion* or *leporello* book, spread to Japan and Korea, and was used for over 1,000 years. The oldest concertina still in existence was made in 949 AD.

WARRING LIBRARIES AND
THE INVENTION OF PARCHMENT

Parchment might never have been invented if the library in Alexandria, in Egypt, and the library in Pergamum, in what is now Turkey, had not been competing to be the library with more scrolls. Around 200 BC, the library in Alexandria had 400,000 papyrus scrolls; Pergamum threatened to make its library larger, so the Egyptians cut off the supply of papyrus to Pergamum. Necessity then forced the library in Pergamum to find a new writing material.

This need prompted the invention of preparing parchment from a thin layer of sheep- or goatskin, which had been scraped with pumice and treated. Calfskin produced an even higher-quality parchment known as *vellum*. Both vellum and parchment were more expensive than papyrus, but they had significant advantages that outweighed the expense. Neither material tore easily, and both sides could be used for writing, whereas only one side of papyrus could be used.

However, parchment and vellum also presented challenges. Because the materials could not be joined effectively into long strips to make scrolls, several sheets were folded down the middle and sewn together through the fold; this became another precursor of the modern book. Also, as humidity rose and fell, parchment tended to warp and buckle, which could twist and distort the books. To counteract this, rigid covers were made of wood wrapped in leather, and the books were held shut by clasps across their edges. This held the pages flat, as in a press. Because codices could be opened to any page in the text, and a larger text could be bound as a unit, parchment and vellum codices gradually replaced the papyrus scroll.

COPTIC BINDING

In the second or third century AD, the Copts, early Christians living in Egypt, developed the Coptic binding. They folded a few sheets of papyrus together into sections. Then, adapting their technique of interlacing threads in carpetmaking and weaving, they used a chain stitch to bind the sections between wooden covers. Once parchment became available, it quickly replaced papyrus for the pages. This binding technique was used throughout the Islamic world and Eastern Christendom (Europe), and is still used in Ethiopia today. By the fall of Rome, in 476 AD, parchment had largely replaced papyrus, except in Egypt.

MEDIEVAL SCRIPTORIA

With the onset of the Dark Ages in Europe, nearly all bookmaking stopped, and many libraries closed. By the 600s, book production continued only in areas where Christianity flourished. Handwritten manuscripts were copied and *illuminated* (illustrated) by hand in Christian monasteries. This was the main activity of monks and some nuns in Europe—particularly Wales, England, and Ireland—but also in parts of Asia and Africa. The monks worked from dawn to dusk six days a week, in special rooms called *scriptoria*, which faced the sun. Because of the possibility of fire, with so many valuable manuscripts in one area, no candles were used for light, nor stoves for heat, even in winter. The scribes themselves often did their own binding, and their work reached a high standard in the 700s in Ireland.

❍ SEWING ONTO CORDS

The late eighth and early ninth centuries saw an improvement in binding techniques. Sections were now sewn onto cords, and the cords were attached to cover *boards*. This added support made the binding more durable.

Because of the cost of materials and labor—one copy of a book could take years to produce—books were prohibitively expensive and usually were commissioned only by educated royalty and upper-class nobles. From the 800s to the 1200s, some of these nobles commissioned *treasure bindings* (see fig. 1–5)—covers decorated with panels of ivory, metal, tooled leather, or gems.

1–4 Girdle books containing hymns, ceremonies, and prayers were carried by monks; the braided knob slid under their belt, or girdle, to hold the book in place. The one shown was written and bound in 1454 for the monastery of Kastl, near Nuremberg, in Germany. Covers are doeskin over wooden boards, with metal clasps and strips of leather. *Girdle book,* closed, Spencer Collection, MS 39; 4 5/16 x 2 15/16 x 3 1/4" (11 x 7.5 x 8.3 cm); height including

leather cover and knot: 8 15/16" (22.7 cm). Photo by Robert D. Rubic. Courtesy of the New York Public Library; Astor, Lenox, and Tilden foundations.

1–5 The front cover of this repoussé treasure binding book has silver filigree, gem mounts, and a tooled rim. Inside, an illuminated Latin manuscript documents correct church procedures for the Weingarten Abbey in Germany, c. 1220–1245. The binding is of pink leather over wooden boards sewn on three double thongs. Size: 9 1/2 x 7 x 3 3/4" (24.5 x 18 x 9.5 cm). Courtesy of the Trustees of the Pierpont Morgan Library, New York. M.711, FC.

CHAINED LIBRARIES

In the late Middle Ages, from 1300 to the 1450s, the heavy wooden cover boards for books were still necessary because of the parchment pages and the handling most books received in the monasteries and colleges. Attached to the cover of each book was a chain, which, in turn, was attached to the table or sloping shelf on which the book was displayed. This prevented the theft of valuable manuscripts. Because of the chains and the durable bindings of these books, many still exist. In later years, durability was sacrificed to faster production and lower costs.

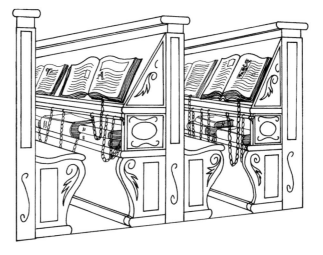

A chained-book library

PAPER REPLACES PARCHMENT

Though the Chinese managed to keep their papermaking techniques secret for several hundred years, the process eventually reached Iraq by 800 and Egypt by 900. In Europe, paper was made in Spain in 1100, in Italy in 1275, and in England by 1490. In the 1200s, paper for books began to replace the more expensive parchment. By the 1400s, paper manuscripts were common. Because paper warped less than parchment, the clasps (except for decorative purposes) and heavy wooden cover boards were no longer needed.

MOVABLE TYPE

In 868, the Chinese achieved the printing of images and type carved into woodblocks. The hand-printed Buddhist scripture *The Diamond Sutra* was probably the first book ever printed. In 1045, the Chinese printer Bi Sheng made the first movable type. Each clay character was made in reverse, and the characters were arranged to spell out a text. In 1250, movable bronze type was invented in Korea, but movable type in China and Korea never flourished because the language of each nation had far too many characters to make the process practical. Not until 1450 did the use of movable type develop further, possibly because all Western words are spelled from only twenty-six letters.

⊚ THE PRINTING PRESS

The invention of the first printing press is credited to Johannes Gutenberg, in Mainz, Germany, in 1450. The press was adapted from a machine that pressed grapes and cheese. Because Gutenberg used movable metal type, letters could be rearranged; and printers could produce 300 impressions a day. The first printed book was the Bible, completed in 1455.

Printed books soon replaced hand-copied books, though they were greeted with suspicion at first: some people thought that printing was a black art, their only explanation for how books could be produced so quickly. With increased availability and lower prices, books became affordable to many people for the first time, and the new industry boomed. By 1500, there were over 1,000 printers in Europe. Books were printed in many languages, not just classical Latin. This led to an increase in the exchange of information and ideas and the development of new inventions, the hallmarks of the Renaissance.

1–6 The front cover of this bible features a portrait of Prince Charles, who later became King Charles II. It is bound in satin that is elaborately embroidered with gold thread and spangles. The images on both covers are worked in silk thread in recessed ovals. *English Bible with embroidered cover,* 1644. Anonymous embroiderer, printed by Tom Barker, London. Open as shown: 6 3/16 x 7 1/2" (15.5 x 19 cm). Closed: 6 x 3 1/2 x 1 3/4" (15.5 x 9 x 4.6 cm). Ties are made of gold cloth. By permission of the Houghton Library, Harvard University.

THE IMPACT OF THE PRINTED WORD

With the invention of printing, the need for books to be copied by hand gradually ended, putting many copyists and illuminators out of work. Because more books were available, increasing numbers of people could read and write.

Although printing made possible the quick production of many books, the supply of handmade paper was limited. Handmade paper, in turn, was limited by the supply of linen and cotton rags used for pulp. In 1719, René de Réamur, a Frenchman, figured out how to process wood from trees to make paper pulp. Although this new paper did not last as long as rag papers or parchment, its development resulted in an increased supply of papermaking material. Now the primary limitation on book production was the speed at which paper could be made by hand.

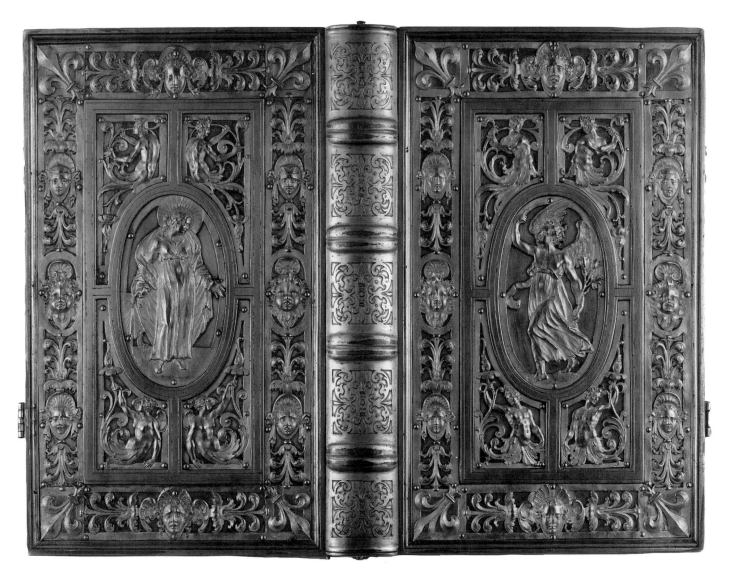

1–7 These covers are made of silver with recessed compartments in which panels of low-relief gilt silver are riveted in place. Two central oval panels depict the Annunciation, with the virgin on the left and the angel on the right. The book has a plain vellum binding, and was the most famous manuscript of the Italian High Renaissance. Antonio Gentili (Italian), *The Farnese Hours,* c. 1591–1609. Silver, vellum, 7 1/4 x 4 1/2 x 1 3/16" (18.5 x 11.5 x 3 cm), when closed. Courtesy of the Trustees of the Pierpont Morgan Library, New York. M69, FC, spine, BC.

MECHANIZED PAPERMAKING
AND BOOKMAKING

A papermaking machine was invented in France in 1799, but it was not until 1804, in England, that a paper mill used such a machine. Its expanded use dramatically increased the paper supply and lowered its cost, which further reduced the price of books. As papermaking, printing, and binding methods improved, books were printed more quickly. This lowered labor costs, and the price of books dropped again. The demand for and the production of books expanded because literacy rose (due to public education).

The industrial revolution changed bookmaking completely. Lithography was discovered in 1798. The first steam-powered cylinder press was built in 1811. In 1884, the first typesetting machine, the Linotype, was invented. In 1887, it was improved on with the invention of the Monotype machine, which did away with the tedious job of setting each letter of type by hand. The Fotosetter, of 1947, was the first typesetting machine that used a photographic process instead of metal type. All this new equipment forced printing, papermaking, bookbinding, and publishing to become separate, specialized fields.

In 1825, case-bound multisection books were first made. These called for more specialization in production because the cover was made separately from the *text pages*; cover and page sections were joined afterward. Machines for folding the paper and sewing the sections sped up binding. The development of new adhesives, including *PVA* and hot glues, meant that single sheets could be bound together without sewing, which allowed paperbacks to be made. The demand for classically trained bookbinders, and hand-papermakers, declined. Their professions faded, as did respect for handcrafts.

Spearheading a return to simplicity and elegance in design, William Morris and some like-minded individuals in England formed the Arts and Crafts Movement. In about 1880, in response to the mechanization of book production, Morris and his wife, Janie, began to revive handcrafted books. They opened the Kelmscott Press, which featured books with beautiful papers and *typography,* and well-crafted hand-binding. This consciousness of the book as both functional and artistic was the basis for a more recent revival. In the 1970s people began to explore further both the technical and creative aspects of papermaking, printing, and binding, giving rise to a new perspective on books and cards.

GREETING CARDS

VALENTINES

Valentines were probably the first greeting cards ever sent. The name "valentine" may come from a third-century Roman priest of that name. The priest was martyred during the persecution of the Christians and later was declared a saint. Our current celebration in honor of St. Valentine, with the exchange of messages and gifts between loved ones, comes from medieval times. February 14 was chosen for the holiday because of a traditional English belief that the fourteenth is the first day in spring that birds choose their mates.

Paper valentines appeared in the 1500s; by the 1800s, they were mass-produced woodcut prints and lithographs. The French valentines were decorated paper hearts with lace. In the United States—where valentines first became popular during the 1860s, with the absence of loved ones at war—the early valentines were decorated with ornaments of spun glass, mother of pearl, and satin ribbons.

CHRISTMAS CARDS

John C. Horsley, a British illustrator who designed a black-and-white lithographed postcard that was then handpainted in color, is usually credited with the making of the first Christmas card, which was sent as an expression of goodwill in the early 1840s. The card, with an image of a family Christmas dinner and the message "A Merry Christmas and a Happy New Year," was commissioned by Sir Henry Cole. A thousand copies were printed and sold. By the 1860s, Christmas cards were popular, and the practice of sending them had spread through Europe. Christmas cards were first printed in the United States (Massachusetts) in 1875 by Louis Prang, and they caught on as quickly as they had in Europe. Now, millions of Christmas cards are sent yearly, and many other occasions—birthdays, weddings, deaths, and even divorces—are acknowledged with cards.

1–8 Although most Christmas cards today are mass-produced, these handmade cards are reminiscent of an earlier time. Traditional gold tassels and classic Christmas colors are used in a series of cards with cut windows that reveal a greeting. Jean G. Kropper (Australia), *Three Christmas Cards,* 1995, 6 x 4 1/8" (15 x 10.5 cm), commercial papers, charms, gold tassels, embroidery thread. Calligraphy by Olive Bull.

1–9 This handmade Valentine is decorated with a gold, paper lace harp, a common Valentine motif, whose strings are ornamented with tiny beads. Cut-out windows reveal a short note inscribed inside the card. *Handmade Valentine,* c. 1860, approx. 10 x 8" (25.4 x 20.3 cm), white and gold paper lace, plain paper, fabric flowers, beads. Courtesy American Antiquarian Society.

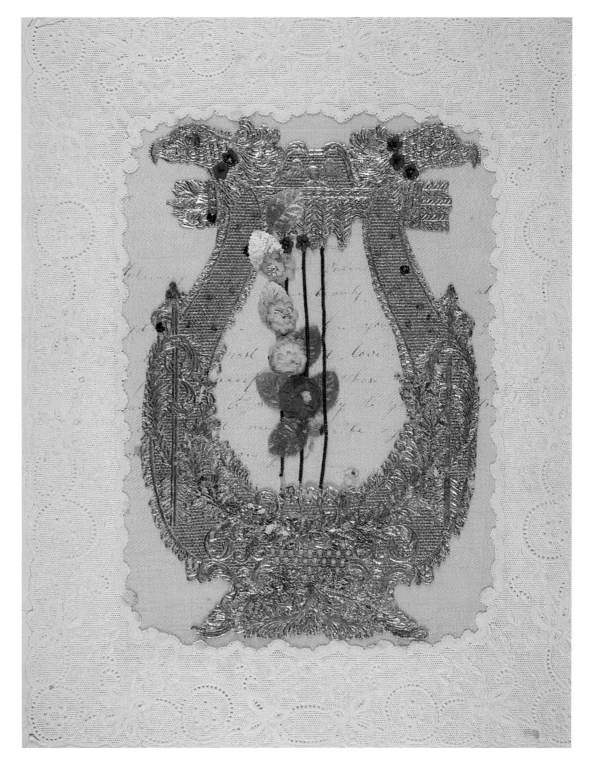

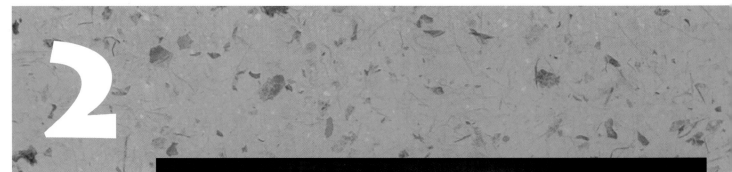

2

2–1 This unique bookwork contains a poem by the artist about how ideas develop. It has 24 pages with a multiple-section binding. Karen Kunc (United States), *Open Book,* 1992. Acrylic, graphite, foil lettering, wood, leather thongs, 12 x 5 x 5" (30.5 x 12.5 x 12.5 cm), when closed.

2–2 These tools are among those most commonly used in bookbinding. Left to right by row, they are: triangle; curved needles for Coptic binding, straight needles for other bindings, linen thread, and an eraser; an awl; a glue stick; a stencil brush for applying PVA glue; a bone folder; a craft knife with protective cap; scissors; pencils; a metal ruler; different-sized punches for creating holes for album and Japanese stab bindings; a small hammer; and beeswax for waxing threads.

TECHNIQUES, TOOLS, AND MATERIALS

To make cards and books, you must cut and fold paper accurately. To do so, you need some basic tools. As you work on various projects throughout this book, you may want to refer to this chapter for general information about procedures and tools.

MAKING THE CUTS

MARKING AND SCORING

A TRIANGLE (also called a *set square*) is used for marking right-angle (90°) corners before cutting. The right angle of a triangle is the corner that fits neatly into any corner of a standard, rectangular sheet of paper.

When you start cutting your own paper, it takes practice to produce straight edges and right-angle corners. Always use a triangle to check your angles before cutting. Using a 30°-60°-90° triangle, place one side of the right-angle along a straight paper edge, and the other side down the page, where you want to cut. Mark along this side with a pencil. Never use the triangle for cutting; the blade will gouge the edge, which ruins the triangle for drawing straight lines.

Later in this book, you will also make a 45°-angle cut. Using a 45°-45°-90° triangle, line up the right-angle side with an outside edge of the paper, and slide the triangle toward the corner until the 45° side is the correct distance from the cover board. Then mark your cutting line.

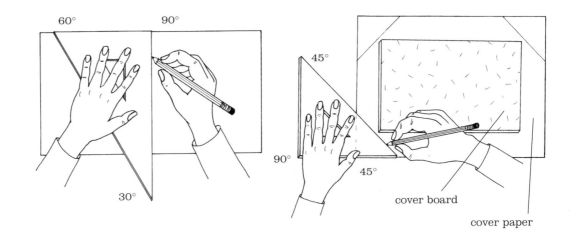

A BONE FOLDER is used to fold paper accurately, *emboss*, score, and make sharp creases. A *bone folder* is shaped somewhat like a tongue depressor, with one end pointed but not sharp. The tools come in different sizes, and are made of bone or polished wood.

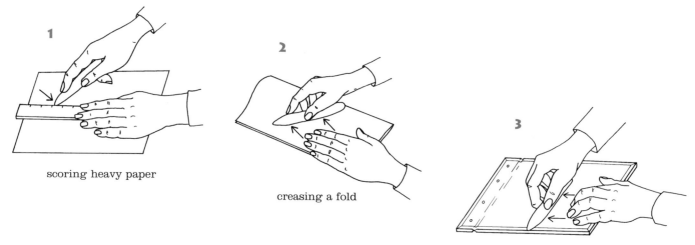

scoring heavy paper

creasing a fold

smoothing pasted papers

1 *Scoring.* To get a clean crease, heavy papers *must* be scored before folding. To score a fold, line up one edge of the ruler with where you want the fold. Hold the bone folder as you would a pencil—pointed end down, with the flat side in line with the fold. Draw the point of the tool along the ruler's edge, pressing down, to score along the inside of the fold. This compresses the fibers of the paper to create a clean line when it is creased.

2 *Creasing.* Leaving the ruler in position, fold the paper loosely along the scored line. Remove the ruler; then fold the paper over, lining up the corners. Run the side of the bone folder along the fold to get a clean crease. The back of a plastic hair comb can substitute for a bone folder for this purpose.

3 *Smoothing.* When you glue or paste papers, press one of the long edges of the bone folder along the length of the papers to smooth the sheets together. This forces out any air bubbles and helps the papers adhere.

A METAL RULER with some thickness, or with a strip of cork underneath, is the safest ruler to use because its upper surface stays above the paper, making it harder for the knife to ride up and cut you. After repeated use, metal rulers remain accurate, undamaged by the gouges that can be made on wooden and plastic rulers.

SPRING-LOADED DIVIDERS measure a distance that you want to match elsewhere. Use only dividers that you can set into position. A compass may be used in place of dividers.

BENCH HOOKS AND CUTTING MATS

If you have a bench hook, you can improve the accuracy of your cutting line. A simple tool that helps hold papers square and gives you something to press or measure against, a bench hook is a board, ideally 11 x 17" (28 x 43 cm). There is one thin strip of wood underneath, and another, which forms a ridge, on the top.

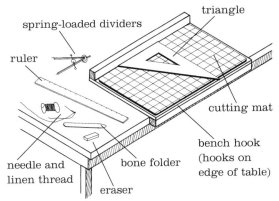

To use a bench hook, press one of the straight edges of your paper against the back ridge. Then lay the triangle on top and press one right-angle side against the ridge, with the other right-angle side running across the paper where you want to mark your cutting line. (See illustration.) This stabilizes the paper and triangle for an accurate measurement.

You can place a *cutting mat* over the bench hook so that after marking your paper, you can pull it clear from the ridge and then cut. Although expensive, a self-sealing cutting mat, because it seals itself back together, provides a cutting surface that does not fall apart after many cuts. Cardboard may be substituted, but ridges and grooves left after cutting make future cuts less accurate.

KNIVES AND CUTTING TOOLS

Craft knives (also called X-acto knives) and rotary cutters are available from craft stores. Be sure to use a knife with blades that you can replace daily, or when the edge becomes blunt; if a blade is not sharp, your work will have irregular and ragged edges. Note that a rotary cutter is particularly good on handmade papers because its blade does not drag. Also have a good, sharpened pair of scissors on hand for trimming corners, threads, or other materials.

WARNING
The most important safety measure to take when you are using cutting tools is to pay careful attention. Stop cutting when someone talks to you or if you become distracted. Dispose of knife blades appropriately and safely; wrap used blades twice in masking tape before discarding.

2–3 Cutting paper with a craft knife.

2–4 Cutting paper with a rotary cutter.

After marking lightly in pencil where you want to cut, use one hand to line up the metal ruler to the marks, being sure your fingers are out of the way. In your other hand, hold the knife like a pen, press down firmly, and draw the blade toward you, keeping it at a 90° angle to the surface of the paper. To cut through cardboard or a stack of papers, use several passes of the knife. Paper cutters, or guillotines, can be used to cut several pieces of paper. Because cutting paper and boards accurately is difficult for beginners or young students, teachers may cut paper before class or provide paper cut to size.

 ## HARD AND SOFT EDGES

You may not think of the edge of a book as a surface, but it is—a surface created by the sum of the page edges. When you make your own books, you have a choice about the appearance of their edges. You can make a *hard edge* by cleanly cutting the edges of each sheet; you can make an irregular *soft edge*, like the deckle edge on handmade paper, by tearing the paper along a ruler, or using a letter opener along the inside of a fold.

2–5 The irregular deckle edges of the paper give this book a soft, textured look. Mary-Lise Beausire (Switzerland), *Journal Intime Avril 1993*, 1993. Handmade paper from iris leaves, 14 x 19 11/16 x 5" (36 x 50 x 13 cm).

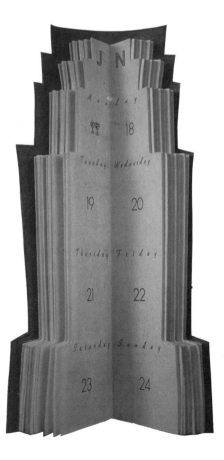

2–6 The hard edges of these shaped (die-cut) pages echo the hard lines of city buildings. Esther K. Smith and Dikko Faust of Purgatory Pie Press (United States), *Skyscraper Datebook*, 1989. Letterpress-printed on elephant hide paper, pop-up endpapers, beads, leather, 9 3/8 x 2 3/8 x 3/8" (23.8 x 6 x .9 cm), when closed.

PUNCHING HOLES

AN AWL, a compass with a sharp point, or a large, sharp needle can be used for piercing holes in papers for binding. Because the awl has a handle, it is easy to use, but each produces equally good results.

A LEATHER HOLE PUNCH, hit with a small hammer, creates (or punches) clean round holes in covers or in a pile of papers. Use the hole punch when the holes will be visible, as in Japanese stab, crossed-ribbon, or hardcover album binding. (See page 69.)

AN ELECTRIC DRILL is used for piercing holes if you don't have a punch. It is best used for holes that aren't visible, because it leaves a rough edge. Protect the papers to be drilled with a sheet of scrap paper on the top and at the bottom of the stack. Use the top sheet as the master template to mark where the holes will be drilled. Place the papers to be drilled between two scrap wooden boards, and check that the papers are square. Clamp this sandwich to a benchtop with two C-clamps, with the top board just back from the holes. Drill with a small drill bit, 1/8" or 3 mm diameter. *If you are not familiar with power tools, always ask for help.* (See page 70.)

BINDING IT TOGETHER

THREAD: Unbleached linen thread is strong and durable, and is the thread most commonly used by bookbinders. Some fabric shops and leatherwork shops carry it, as do bookbinders' suppliers. The marking "16/2" designates the thickness and number of strands in a thread correct for most bookbinding jobs. Numbers 10 to 12 heavy cotton thread, buttonhole thread, cotton crochet thread, carpet thread, and embroidery thread in cotton or silk are reasonable substitutes in most cases.

For thin papers, use a thin linen or silk embroidery thread; a thick one will make the binding bulky. For heavy or thick papers, use a thicker thread; a thin thread will rip through the paper. For coptic binding, use beeswax to strengthen the thread.

NEEDLES: Traditional bookbinding *needles* have slightly blunt points, which prevents ripping through the paper during binding. The needles should be long with an eye the same width as the needle. A bookbinding, darning, or blunt tapestry needle will also do. Sharper needles such as crewel, embroidery (sharps), straw, or milliner's needles (sizes 3 to 9) are used for piercing holes before sewing or when thinner needles are needed.

ANCHORING A THREAD: When binding books, the thread may separate from the needle. This can be avoided by first anchoring the thread, a technique particularly useful for multisection bindings.

1   Split the fibers of the thread with the needle.

2   Push the thread up to the eye.

3   Pull the end of the thread to get rid of the loop. Sew as usual.

PVA (WHITE GLUE)

PVA, or polyvinyl acetate (white glue), is a multipurpose adhesive. Less moist than *paste*, it does not soak into paper. It works mostly on the surface, adhering within ten to fifteen minutes, depending on humidity. Although you have little time to work, and papers can rarely be repositioned, the quick drying time can be an advantage: papers warp less when glued than when pasted, though they still need to be pressed or put under a weight while drying. PVA stays flexible when dry, and is not reversible (once dry, it won't disintegrate if it later gets wet). Glue referred to in this book means PVA glue.

Note that the white glue commonly available in the United States is not PVA glue. It will work, but is less reliable should the book get damp. Check the contents of any glue to be sure it is PVA.

HOW TO APPLY: To glue a piece of paper, lay out newspaper on the work surface. Put the item to be glued facedown on the newspaper. Using a round stencil brush with short, stiff bristles, dip the brush into the PVA and wipe off the excess.

Do not paint or stroke PVA onto the paper; you must pound or "bang" it. This forces the glue into the fibers of the paper to create a stronger bond. Because the bristles of the brush are flat-ended, the brush can be pounded without damage. Always working from the center out, pound the glue into the paper using the stencil brush held vertically. Go over the edges, onto the newspaper, to ensure that the edges will adhere properly. Never draw the brush along the edge because glue will get onto the underside of the paper. *Do not smooth out the glue.* Pick the paper straight up, flip it over, and place it in position on your book or card. Put a piece of nonstick paper over it. Then burnish, or rub down, the paper with the side of a bone folder. This will remove any air bubbles, wrinkles, or excess glue and will help the paper adhere. Discard the (gluey) nonstick paper.

Wrap the work in nonstick paper, then in newspaper, and put your work under a weight or in the press until dry. After pressing, throw out the newspaper, which will have glue on it, so that glue will not get on anything else.

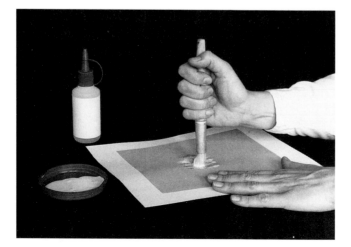

2–7 Applying PVA glue with a stencil brush by pounding it into the fibers of the paper. Photo: E. Lancaster.

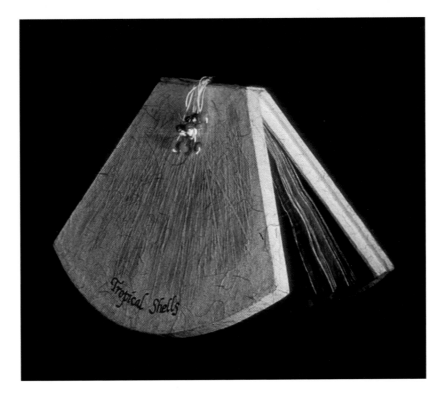

2–8 Paste papers are made by mixing water-based paint or ink into paste (thinned with water), then painting a thin layer on paper. Patterns are made by dragging various tools through the paste. Nancy Pobanz (United States), *Tropical Shells,* 1990. Handmade paste paper, paste painting, linen thread, beads, calligraphy, 6 x 6 x 1/2" (15.2 x 15.2 x 1.3 cm).

 ## PASTE

Paste contains more moisture than PVA. This moisture seeps into the paper, penetrating the fibers to create a strong bond. Paste is completely reversible (rewet pasted papers can be separated again) and it takes longer to dry, but this gives you plenty of time to position papers as you work. Hold the paste brush like a pencil, and work from the center with a sweeping movement. Because there is moisture in the paste, there is the potential for warping as the paste dries. To prevent warping, always wrap newly pasted and burnished books or cards in nonstick paper and then in absorbent paper, and press while drying overnight.

PASTE RECIPE: Although you can buy paste from bookbinding suppliers, you can also make your own. You will need one part white flour to five-to-six parts water. For a smoother whiter paste, use corn flour or rice flour.

Making paste is a bit like making gravy. Mix the flour with one-and-one-half parts cold water until all the lumps are gone; pour through a strainer if necessary. Add the rest of the water, and slowly bring to a gentle boil on medium heat, preferably in a double boiler. Stir continuously once the paste is hot, and cook another

2–9 Applying paste with a soft, long-haired brush. Photo: E. Lancaster.

five minutes. The mixture will thicken to the consistency of heavy cream. A few drops of clove or tea-tree oil can be stirred in as a preservative. Pour the paste into a clean jar, and cover the surface with plastic or waxed paper to prevent a skin from forming and to help preserve the paste. Seal with a lid, and allow the paste to cool. It will keep in the refrigerator for up to two weeks. Never put any paste back into the jar; this introduces bacteria and spoils the paste. If the paste becomes too thick to use, put it in the microwave on medium power (without the lid) for ten to thirty seconds (depending on the amount of paste and the power of the microwave), or reheat it in a saucepan on the stovetop on low heat to soften. Stir in extra water as needed.

A MIX OF GLUE AND PASTE

If you find PVA dries too fast for you, especially in warm weather, experiment with a mixture of two parts glue and one part paste. This combines the qualities of both PVA glue and paste.

GLUE STICK

Use a glue stick for adhering thin papers and small objects on the front of a card, but note that a glue stick provides only a weak surface adhesive. Papers glued with glue sticks do not need to be pressed because there is little moisture in them, and they will not warp as they dry. Glue sticks are easy to use, and some are acid-free.

BRUSHES

A ROUND STENCIL BRUSH, used for applying PVA glue, is made of short, stiff pig's bristle (5/8 x 1") and has a flat end suitable for pounding glue onto paper. Keep these brushes separate from those used for paste.

A PASTE BRUSH is also made from pig's bristle (1/2" round or 3/4" flat, and 1 1/2" long). The brush's long, flexible bristles and the rounded end hold paste well, and are ideal for gently brushing paste onto papers. To preserve any brush, clean and air-dry it thoroughly after use.

PROTECTING YOUR WORK

NONSTICK PAPER, when referred to in this book, means waxed paper, or glassine. Waxed paper is inexpensive and sold in supermarkets. Glassine may be purchased from a bookbinding or photographic supplier.

Wrap nonstick paper around cards and books after pasting or gluing, before putting them in the press. This prevents the PVA glue or paste from seeping out onto other work in the press or onto the press itself. Next, wrap the card or book in absorbent paper, such as newspaper. This absorbs the moisture from the paste or glue *through* the nonstick paper, and helps prevent warping as the work dries.

A PAPERWEIGHT makes your job easier by leaving your hands free. It also prevents your valuable papers from sliding to the floor and possibly becoming damaged.

☘ PRESSING MATTERS

A BOOK PRESS or two boards and two C-clamps are critical tools for book-making. When gluing or pasting papers, press them tightly in a press and release them immediately (referred to as *nipping*) to ensure a good bond. This forces out any air bubbles and puts the two surfaces in full contact. After pasting or gluing large areas, put your work in a press overnight, which helps prevent warping. An alternative is a pile of heavy books, or a board with weights on top.

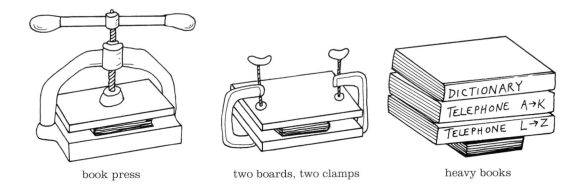

book press   two boards, two clamps   heavy books

PAPER

WEIGHT

The *weight* of paper is measured in pounds (lb) or in grams per square meter (gsm). This measurement is based on the weight of a ream (500 sheets) in a basic size for a specific kind of paper. Book papers (text, offset, opaque, etc.) generally weigh 20–115 lb (30–170 gsm), and cover paper is usually 50–150 lb (135–406 gsm). These weights can be misleading, however—an individual sheet of 70 lb *text paper* is thinner and lighter than a 70 lb sheet of cover paper.

Select a paper with the correct weight (or thickness) for the book's use and size. A paper with a rough surface would not be suitable for stationery but might be perfect for a book cover. A soft handmade paper would not work in a Coptic binding, because the sewing would rip out, but it would work well in a Japanese stab binding or as a page in an album. When you choose paper for a book or card, think about the weight, opacity, stiffness, *grain direction*, *sizing*, texture, pattern, and color you need.

For book covers, cardboard (sometimes referred to as *board* or *greyboard*) of varying weight and thickness is used. Thicker cardboard is generally used for larger books. *Archivite* is a dense cardboard made for bookbinding.

⊛ GRAIN

When paper is manufactured commercially, a watery solution of pulp and water is sprayed onto a moving belt of stainless steel mesh. The fibers line up parallel to the direction of the moving mesh, giving the paper a grain direction. Folding paper parallel to the grain and between the fibers is easier than folding across the grain, and will produce cleaner, stronger folds. Paper folded across the grain gives an irregular line and is likely to crack with use.

The grain of the paper should always be parallel to the spine in books; and in cards, parallel to the fold. This ensures that the binding is not stressed as the paper expands and contracts with changes in humidity and temperature.

There are two techniques for finding grain direction.

1   First, try tearing the paper along one side. If it tears easily and fairly straight, that is the direction of the grain. If it tears in a jagged line diagonally across the page, that is the direction against the grain. Grain direction is more pronounced in some papers than in others.

arrows indicate
grain direction

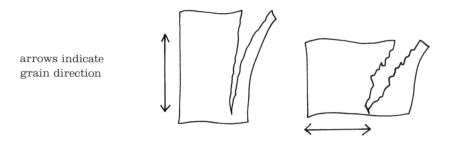

2   The second method of finding grain is called *bouncing*. Bend the paper in half, but do not crease it. Shut your eyes, press down gently on the paper, and notice how much "bounce," or resistance, it has. Open your eyes, open out the paper, turn it 90°, and bend it the other way. Close your eyes, bounce the paper, and feel the resistance. Which way has less resistance to the bouncing? The bending that gives less resistance is parallel to the grain. In light pencil, mark this direction on the paper with a double-headed arrow. When folded against the grain, the paper resists bending because you are trying to bend the fibers themselves rather than bending *between* the fibers.

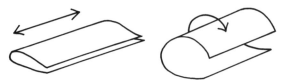

2–10 Collage cards can tell stories or just be an arrangement of things that are pleasing to the eye. Aggrey Chilemba (Malawi), 1995. Recycled hand-made paper, dried plants, seed pods, and guinea fowl feathers, 6 x 4 1/8" (15.24 x 10.5 cm) and 4 1/8 x 6" (10.5 x 15.24 cm).

2–11 Papers made with unusual plant fibers add texture to this single-section artist's book. Susan Kapuscinski Gaylord (United States), *Spirit Book #1: Sewn Prayer,* 1992. Mexican bark paper, Chinese joss paper, handmade paper from Bhutan, coconut disks, and gold thread, on grapevine stand, 5 x 21 x 11" (12.5 x 52.5 x 27.5 cm).

ALTERNATIVE AND RECYCLED FIBERS FOR PAPERMAKING

Currently, the commercial paper industry makes paper primarily from ground wood chips and cellulose fiber from sawmill waste. Surprisingly, trees do not yield the best or the longest fibers for papermaking, and they take many years to grow. Other plants—hemp, sugar cane, and hibiscus—are more efficient sources of cellulose fiber, and these will be used more in the future. Paper made from alternative fibers or recycled wood pulp helps preserve natural resources.

ACID-FREE: PAPER MADE TO LAST

If you are producing a book for posterity, such as a photo album, you will need chemically stable *acid-free* or *archival* paper, which is more expensive than other papers. (If you use this kind of paper, also use acid-free PVA glue.) Most paper is not acid-free; if it is not marked "acid free," you can assume it is *not.*

Acidic paper, like newsprint, is not chemically stable. You have probably noticed how old newspapers turn yellow and brittle. This is because the paper is breaking down chemically. If you are designing a book that needs to last 50 years, do not use newsprint. Copy paper and drawing paper are of good quality, but are not acid-free. These papers form the middle ground and will last 20 years if kept away from direct sun or high humidity.

HANDMADE PAPER

Throughout this book are examples of works made from handmade papers. When you make handmade paper, you decide such properties as color, size, surface texture, and sizing—all of which add personality to cards and books. The fiber that you use for handmade paper can be made from newly cut trees ground into woodchips (called virgin pulp), pulp recycled from used wood-pulp papers, or pulp prepared directly from plants other than trees. If you purchase handmade or recycled paper, ask about the paper's properties. What fibers were used? Is it recycled? Is it well suited for a particular purpose? Is it sized?

SIZING

Sizing is a chemical that is added to paper pulp; it fills in the gaps between the fibers of the paper to make it stronger and less absorbent. Writing or painting on sized paper does not *bleed*, or fan out into a thick spidery line. If you intend to use paper for painting, writing with a felt-tip pen, calligraphy, or photographic prints, the paper must first be sized. Knowing how to size your own paper gives you a larger choice of papers to use for your cards and books.

Use either *methyl cellulose* (the kind without fungicide) or a packet of gelatin, mixed according to the accompanying directions. You may also use one part corn flour with six parts water, cooked slowly, like gravy, to make a thin paste. Use a wide soft paintbrush to apply a thin, even layer of the solution of choice over the paper, and leave it to dry. Apply a second thin coat, and leave that to dry. Do the same to the other side of the paper. If you use gelatin, put the warm liquid mixture into a rectangular cake pan. Then dip individual papers into the pan. The sized paper dries in a few hours or up to a day, depending on the humidity.

2–12 After learning how to make the bindings in this book, you can experiment and design your own, as the artist has in this forty-page book in an original binding. This sculptural piece is permanently open, sealed in a plexiglass box. Wim de Vos (Australia), *Threads, Marks, Remarks—Time Lost, Time Gained*, 1995. Engraved polycarbonate pages in an acrylic box, black cotton thread, 2 3/8 x 12 3/4 x 5 3/4" (6 x 32.5 x 14.7 cm). Photo: Adèle Outteridge.

2–13 Inventive in her use of unusual materials, the artist of this book has created a modern version of the treasure bindings made from 800 to 1200, which were decorated with gems, ivory, and precious metals (back cover shown). Barbara Mauriello (United States), *Jeweled Binding,* 1992. Leather over wood, 23-karat gold, silk embroidery, and glass buttons, 6 1/4 x 5 1/2 x 2" (15.6 x 13.1 x 5 cm).

UNUSUAL MATERIALS

Unusual materials can add a distinctive look to cards and books. If the materials are relevant, they can help support the message of the work. Possibilities for materials to use include fur, tapa, plant-fiber papers, weaving, sheet metal, Plexiglas™, wood and wood veneer, birch bark, velvet, and wire. See what materials are available and how they might relate to your subject.

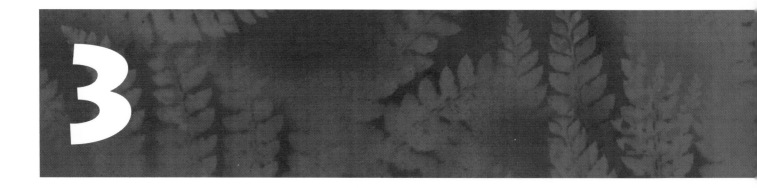

3

3–1 Type and illustration work together to give this dynamic piece its power. Adrian Tió Díaz (United States), *El Manipulador,* 1990. Letterpress-printed broadside on hand-pigmented paper, 24 x 18" (61 x 45.7 cm). Bilingual text by Gerry Smith, printed with Russell McKnight at the Logan Elm Press and paper mill, Ohio.

TYPOGRAPHY AND PRINTING

TYPOGRAPHY

Each typeface has a particular character. You might, for instance, select a whimsical typeface for a funny card, or a flowery one for a wedding invitation. Take care to select a typeface that is easy to read and that suits the message of your book or card.

Some typefaces are beautifully ornate, but they are difficult to read. So too are all uppercase letters. Putting a short headline all in uppercase letters is fine, but don't put a large block of type all in uppercase if you want it to be readable. Instead, provide a mix of uppercase and lowercase letters. Using too many typefaces may also be confusing; for a more cohesive look, stick to one or two contrasting typefaces, and use them in different sizes and different weights. Remember, the purpose of typography is to communicate a message clearly and appropriately.

CREATIVE IDEA

Pick a letter, any letter, and go through magazines, books, and newspapers, cutting out all the examples you find of that one letter. Use a glue stick to fix them in rows or a spiral on one page. Notice the different shapes and styles.

VOCABULARY

Certain terms and ways of describing typography may not be familiar to you, but understanding them might be helpful when making decisions about your book or card.

Letterspacing is the space between individual letters. The space between lines of type is called *leading*—when type was set by hand, little strips of lead were inserted between the lines of type to space them out. Both letterspacing and leading can be loose or tight.

Type can also be light or bold (dark), italic (slanted), condensed (narrow), or extended (wide). Some typefaces have serifs, or fine lines on the ends of the letters, but others do not. Therefore, typefaces are described as either *serif* or *sans serif* (without serifs).

The size of letters is measured in *points*. Line length is measured in units called *picas*. If you have access to page layout or word-processing software, you can experiment with typography to see what looks right for your project.

Light type	This is 8-point type.
Bold type	This is 10-point type.
Italic type	This is 12-point type.
Condensed type	This is 16-point type.
Extended type	This is 20-point type.

CARD GREETINGS

When writing greetings for a card, try out various places to divide lines of copy. Effective line breaks contribute to the intent of the message and to visual appeal. Study professional greeting cards and poetry, which generally make good use of line breaks.

WHITE SPACE

White space around type is important. Without it, a page looks cluttered and uninviting. Similar to a mount around a framed picture, which focuses attention and gives importance to the artwork, white space on the page draws the eye to the type. Give your words the space they deserve.

COMBINING TYPE AND IMAGES

You can use typography or imagery alone on a page, or you can combine the two. The artists and authors who have created the most dynamic cards and books have put some thought into how the type and images will work together. Look at the range of examples here, and think about the choices that were made to produce them.

> If you choose a delicate typeface, don't put something with it that will overwhelm; it is a marriage. You can play with the letters until they become part of the design. I like them to be very clear, with lots of space, each letter to make a statement. Sometimes I call my work 'Jeu de lettres' or playing with letters. I arrange them so that each one stands on its own, like in a bunch of flowers, yet never overcrowding. It is a balance. I see it when it works.
>
> —Gérard Charriere,
> Swiss-Trained Typographer and Book Artist

REPRODUCING CARDS AND BOOKS

You can handwrite, draw, or paint both type and imagery for your books and cards, but sometimes you might want a different look. Try linoleum cuts, eraser and woodblock prints, silkscreens, photosensitive polymer plates, etchings, letterpress printing, and photocopies for printing cards and books. Your choice will depend on your skills, the look you want, and your access to equipment. Each technique can be used for reproducing both type and images, and allows you to make one copy or many copies. (*Editioning* is the process of making many identical copies of a book.)

3–3 In this book, type is used as a design element. Letters were cut out, coated with PVA glue, sprinkled with sand, and then coated with black acrylic and metal powders. This book is unique or one-off, meaning only one was made. Gérard Charriere (United States), *Sand Alphabet,* 1989. Hand-painted type, glue, sand, black acrylic and metal powders, linen cover, leather spine, 11 3/4 x 22 x 2" (29.8 x 55.9 x 5 cm), when closed.

SILKSCREENS

In silkscreening, type or an image is cut into a screen, either photographically or by hand. To print, inks are wiped across the screen; the inks squeeze through the screen and onto the page, producing the shape of the type or image.

BLOCK PRINTS

Linoleum-cut, eraser-cut, and wood block prints are all made in three steps. First, a drawing of the image or type (or both) is made on tracing paper; it is then reversed by flipping the paper over. Then, with the use of carbon paper, the drawing is transferred onto the linoleum, large white eraser, or woodblock. Type and images are reversed (backwards) on the plate.

Next, the surface of the block is prepared by carefully carving out either the area *around* the images and type, or by carving out the images and type themselves. The third step is printing: oil- or water-based ink is rolled on top of the plate with a rubber roller; then the plate is printed onto paper, either by hand or on a press. This again reverses the type and images, making them *right-reading* (meaning that type or images can be read as usual, and are not upside down or backwards).

All these methods are good for bold designs. Erasers are inexpensive, readily available, and can be cut with a craft knife. They are also much softer than linoleum or wood, which makes them easier to carve. However, fewer prints can be made from erasers because they wear away through handling and their surface is easily damaged.

3–4 Working in the bush in central southern Africa, a collective of paper-makers and artists produce cards and books to sell at area markets and to people on safari. Cartolina Handmade Paper (Zimbabwe) *Handmade Maize-Paper Card*, 1995. Silkscreen by Design Incorporated printed on mealie paper from locally-harvested maize plants, mounted on a card of recycled paper, 5 3/4 x 8" (14.5 x 20.7 cm).

3–5 This artist designed a series of three-color linocut prints—bound on the right-hand side of the page—to tell a well-known story from her religious heritage: how the son of Israel got out of Egypt with the leader Moshe, to reach Israel. Ora Lahav-Chaaltiel (Israel), *"Hagada": The Story of Pesach*, 1995. Handmade kozo paper, 11 x 8 x 3/4" (28.8 x 22.3 x 1.8 cm).

3–6 The type for this elegant book of poems was reversed and then carved into a white plastic polymer eraser and printed like a linoleum cut. The carving tools were made by the artist, who inserted slivers from razor blades into the ends of chopsticks that were cut in half. Judith Haswell (New Zealand), *Potsherds and Geraniums*, 1991. Eraser prints, 7 3/8 x 4 3/4 x 1/4" (18.7 x 12 x .6 cm), when closed.

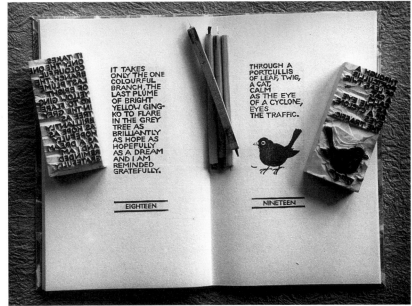

COLLAGRAPHS

Collagraph prints are usually made from thin cardboard plates with images created in one of two ways: The first is collaging (and gluing) items on top. The items collaged must be consistently thin to make it possible to ink and print them evenly. The second technique is to cut reversed images or type into the cardboard and peel up thin layers of the board's surface. The plates are then sealed with shellac (or matte or gloss medium) and allowed to dry.

The plates can be relief printed by inking them with a roller and printing them by hand or on a press, creating an image from the raised areas. Alternately, the plate can be intaglio printed by rubbing ink into the recessed areas and any textures collaged on top. Intaglio printing must be done on a press, which forces the paper into the inked areas (recesses and textures), producing an image with tones of light and dark.

ETCHINGS

Etchings are prints made from zinc or copper plates painted with a protective coating. The image or type is reversed and drawn into the coating. When the plate is submerged into acid, the image is bitten into the plate where the lines were drawn. Ink is rubbed into the recessed areas (intaglio) and printed under pressure on a press.

3–7 A room full of family photos and memories inspired this book, designed as a testament to the death of the artist's great aunt. Amy M. Bay (United States), *Auntie Ree,* 1994. Printed from metal etching plates, 11 3/4 x 8 3/4 x 3/4" (29.4 x 21.9 x 1.9 cm), when closed.

3–8 This design makes good use of white space on the page. Futura, a commercial typeface, is combined with Hebrew type hand lettered by the artist. Lynne Avadenka (United States), *An Only Kid* (edition of 75), 1990. Letterpress-printed pamphlet-bound book, 10 1/4 x 6 7/8 x 1/4" (26 x 17.5 x .63 cm), when closed. Photo: Steve Benson.

 ## PHOTOSENSITIVE POLYMER PLATES

These plates are made of a light-sensitive rubbery plastic. A master is made for each page of type, with images in black. From the master, a photocopy on acetate (or a film positive) is made to fit the plate. The acetate is flipped over, or reversed, and laid on top of the photosensitive plate; a clean sheet of glass is placed on top. This is exposed to sunlight; the plate is then held under running water. The parts of the plate exposed to the sun will wash away, leaving the raised areas where there were type and images. The plate can be printed by hand or on a press.

 ## LETTERPRESS

Letterpress is printing with raised metal type that is inked and pressed onto paper. It has a crisp, clean look, quite distinctive from the more common offset printing. Images and type can be letterpress-printed together. Many book artists use second-hand letterpresses set up at home.

 ## OFFSET PRINTING

Most commercial printing jobs use offset printing because it reproduces detail accurately and is economical for printing large numbers of pieces. This printing technique requires thin, flexible metal or paper plates with flat surfaces, and works on the principle that oil and water do not mix. The area on the plate to be printed—the type and the images—is coated with a material that attracts oil-based inks and repels water. The plate is attached to a cylinder, which is rolled against another cylinder that is wet with water. The first cylinder is then rolled against a cylinder coated with oil-based ink. Ink sticks to the plate only in the type-and-images area. The ink is then transferred, or *offset*, from the inked plate to a soft rubber-blanket cylinder or roller against which the paper is pressed.

PHOTOCOPYING

Photocopying in black and white or color is suitable for some cards and books. Type can be laid out and glued to a sheet of paper page by page (to be used as a master for photocopying) or simply placed facedown directly on the copier. Photographs, black-and-white drawings, patterned papers, fabric, or relatively flat objects can be placed behind the type and copied with it. Photocopying is a quick, easy way to edition your work.

MAKING A CLASS BOOK

A class or group of people can make a book that focuses on a news item, environmental issue, or a theme chosen by the teacher. Each person designs a page, and then all participants work together to reproduce the pages and bind them into a book.

MATERIALS
- white paper, 8 1/2 x 11" (metric A4), for sketching ideas and for the dummy book
- glue sticks
- scissors
- fine and medium black markers
- newspapers and magazines, for collage and for scrap paper
- papers and materials needed for the final books (refer to pages 68–85 for binding techniques and supplies)

DIRECTIONS

1 Brainstorm ideas for the book's theme and discuss what the book will look like. Have participants explain their suggestions to the group, which then makes decisions by a majority vote. Choose the book's title, size, color, shape, and the approximate number of pages.

2 Choose the method of reproduction and the binding, depending on the skills of the group and the equipment available. Photocopying, eraser prints, and lino prints are the easier means of reproduction. Japanese stab, crossed-ribbon, and album bindings are easiest because they are made with single leaves.

3 Make a mock-up, or dummy, of the book, which is helpful for planning and design. Leave pages free at the front for the title page and contents, and a page at the back for a *colophon*, an inscription that tells who worked on the book, who published it, the reproduction technique, and the place and date of publication.

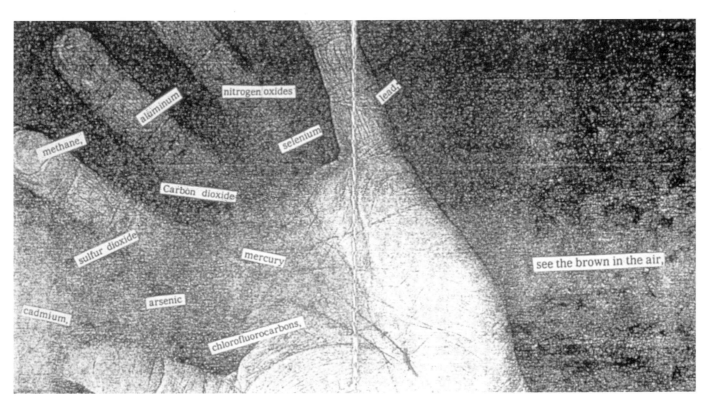

The labels in the image read:

methane,
aluminum
nitrogen oxides
lead,
selenium
Carbon dioxide
sulfur dioxide
mercury
see the brown in the air,
cadmium,
arsenic
chlorofluorocarbons,

3–9 In this twelve-page book, the artist expresses her concern about dire global forecasts. Sharon Gilbert (United States), *Urgent Life* (edition of 300), 1990. Black-and-white electrography (photocopy), news-clip collages, binding sewn on a sewing machine. 4 1/2 x 4 1/8 x 1/2" (11.2 x 10.3 x 1.3 cm), when closed.

4 Decide what will be on each page: only words, only images, words and images, or neither. Choose the typeface (or handwriting) and the style of illustration. You may want to use collaged type and images.

5 Decide who will do what on the project. Participants may work alone or in teams on a particular page or other aspect of the book.

6 Choose how many copies you want to make. Make enough for each group member and for anyone else who might like a copy.

7 Design the pages, make the originals or plates, and reproduce them. Let all work dry thoroughly. Collate the pages, checking that all the copies are the same. Put the covers into place and bind the pages into a book.

8 Look over your results and assess what you have done. What did you learn from the process? Would you handle anything differently next time?

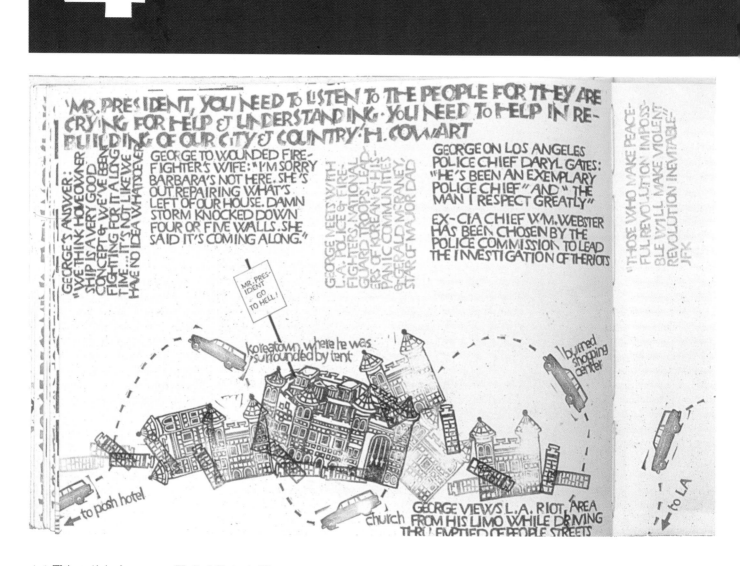

4–1 This satirical piece on former president George Bush includes photos from newspapers, quotations, political rhetoric, and details of Supreme Court appointments. Joan Iversen Goswell (United States), *The George Book*, 1992. Hand-carved eraser stamps, collage, xerography (type and images) in a multisection binding, 9 x 15 x 1" (22.5 x 37.5 x 2.5 cm) when closed.

MAKING PATTERNED PAPERS

For books, patterned paper may be used for covers, *endpapers*, or *flysheets*. For cards, patterned paper may form the whole card, or be cut into shapes to decorate the cover. You can custom-design patterned paper: use plastic-wrap patterned papers for Christmas cards (in red and green) or for Hanukkah cards (in blue and silver), or decorate papers with rubbings of patterns in pinks and reds to make Valentine's Day cards.

 ## CARVED POTATO AND ERASER PRINTS

Printing with stamps is an easy way to build pattern on papers and can be adapted to any age group. Even though some children will be too young to do the carving, they can help with ideas. The simplicity of this technique does not prevent sophisticated results. You can achieve dynamic patterns by carving on potatoes or erasers, and then stamping single images in layers, with pale colors stamped under stronger colors. To make multiple copies of your work, you can offset-print or photocopy paper that has been stamped with black ink.

4–2 Carve your own eraser stamps and use them to make wrapping paper or decorative borders on cards or stationery.

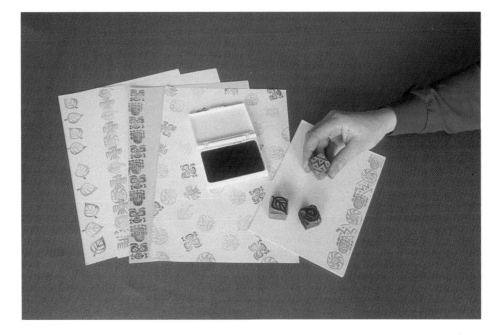

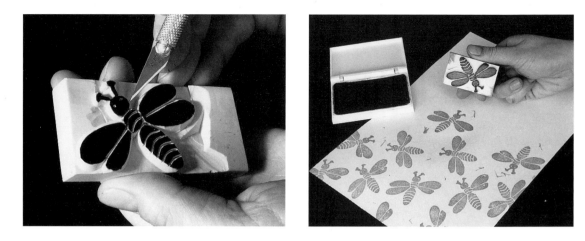

4–3 After designing your stamp, draw the image on the eraser in felt-tip marker and carefully carve away around the image.

4–4 Print your own patterned papers using a stamp pad and your newly carved stamp. Change the orientation of the stamp each time to make the pattern viewable from any direction.

White plastic erasers have a smoother surface and are more suited to printing detail than are brown rubber erasers. To get the texture and workability that you want, try different kinds of erasers. After carving, use the stamp as is, or glue it to a small block of wood with PVA or a solvent-based glue. *Use in a well-ventilated area.*

MATERIALS

- drawing paper
- pencil
- newspaper
- felt-tip marker (medium point)
- a few fresh potatoes cut in half, or some erasers
- craft knife with a new blade, for cutting erasers or potatoes
- sharp paring knife, for cutting potatoes only
- stamp pads or water-based paint (poster paint, gouache, watercolor)
- scrap paper
- nontoxic paints, inks, or washable-ink stamp pads
- brush (any small paintbrush)
- paper, commercial or handmade

Note: Do not use a knife with a serrated blade for carving printing stamps because it will create an uneven printing surface and detract from the image.

DIRECTIONS

1 Sketch your designs on paper, keeping in mind the size of the eraser or potato you will use. Because you will be able to print the stamp—or several different stamps—over and over to form a group of images, make an image of something most often seen in groups: a horse, a leaf, or a car.

2 Spread newspaper on the work surface. Use the marker to draw the image on the eraser. If you are using potatoes, they are too wet to draw on. You can cut freehand or use a paper template cut to the size of the potato. Use the craft knife to cut out the spaces around the image. (See fig. 4–3.)

3 Ink the stamp on a stamp pad, or use the brush to paint color onto the stamp. Experiment on scrap paper. (You can test-print your stamp as you carve.)

4 To create wrapping paper, make an allover pattern, printing the image right side up, upside down, and sideways. This makes the pattern viewable from any angle. (See fig. 4–4.)

5 For distinctive stationery, make border patterns across the top or down the side. Use one color or a combination of several; after the use of each color, clean the stamp by stamping a few times on scrap paper.

6 Gently clean the color off the stamps with soap and water, and dry before storing. Potato stamps will last for a few days if stored in a plastic bag in the refrigerator. The erasers will last for years if stored in a cool place away from direct sunlight.

RUBBINGS

Many surfaces can be rubbed to reproduce their lettering, patterns, or textures. Tiles with a design of raised ridges, mosaics, patterned brick walkways, incised words on monuments and plaques, and raised wood grain on weathered boards all work well. Look for possibilities.

> **MATERIALS**
> - 60–80 lb (120–180 gsm) drawing or photocopy paper
> - jumbo crayons (or paint sticks) of different colors
> - watercolors, inks, or water-based paints (optional)
> - brush (optional)

DIRECTIONS

1 Place a sheet of paper over the surface to be rubbed, and hold it in place with one hand. (The paper must be thin enough to pick up the texture, but heavy enough not to tear.) Hold the crayon sideways, and rub firmly over the surface of the paper to create the pattern. The color will be strongest over the raised areas, and lightest on the depressed areas.

2 Move the paper and do a second rubbing in another color, either on the same texture or a different texture. Turn the paper 90° or slide it sideways.

4–5 Taking rubbings from a textured surface is a simple way to create unusual patterns on papers for use in cards and books. See what surfaces you can find in your environment, such as the textured glass shown here.

3 Continue overlapping rubbings in different colors. Try one rubbing in a light color and the second in a dark color. Experiment.

4 Use these papers as they are, or wash over the crayon with inks or water-based paint. Apply the color thinly with a wet brush. The crayon will resist the paint, but the paint will cover the background.

4–6 Papers decorated with plastic-wrap patterns can be used in creative ways, as shown in these cards and the Coptic-bound book. Jean G. Kropper with calligraphy by Olive Bull (Australia), 1995. Watercolor paper and inks, machine embroidery; cards: 8 x 4" (20 x 10 cm) and 7 1/2 x 3 1/2" (19 x 9 cm); book: 6 1/8 x 4 3/16 x 3/4" (15.5 x 10.6 x 2 cm).

🌲 PLASTIC-WRAP PATTERNS

With this technique—which requires watercolors, gouache, poster paint, or water-based inks—you can create textured abstract patterns. People of any age group can create these.

MATERIALS

- newspaper or sheets of plastic
- a sheet of heavy watercolor or other well-sized paper
- clean rag or paper towel
- eyedropper
- thinned water-based paint (or ink), three or four colors
- plastic wrap
- *optional:* rubber gloves

Note: The paper must be well sized so it will not disintegrate when soaked with water or paint.

DIRECTIONS

1 Protect the work surface with newspaper or plastic. Hold the paper under running water, thoroughly wetting it. Be sure there are no dry spots. Hold the paper by one corner and allow the excess water to drip off; then lay it on the newspaper. Blot dry any puddles of water with a clean rag or paper towel.

2 With the eyedropper, drop the first color randomly over the paper, in separate, spaced-out areas. It is fine if the color puddles. (See fig. 4–7.)

3 Choose a second color and repeat the process. Drop this color between the areas of the first color. Allow puddles to overlap and bleed into one another. If you wish, continue with more colors.

4 Cut a length of plastic wrap twice as long as the paper. Lay the wrap down on top of the paper. Crumple it across the surface of the paper, allowing the ink to creep up into the folds and twists of the plastic. Once crumpled, the plastic will cover a fairly small area. Leave the wrap in place. Cut another length of plastic,

4–7 Use an eyedropper to drop inks or thinned paints randomly onto wet paper. Use different colors, and watch them bleed together.

4–8 Crumple lengths of plastic wrap on the surface of the wet paper to cover it; then leave it to dry completely. The plastic wrap will channel the colors into intriguing abstract patterns. Peel off the plastic after the inks are dry.

and repeat the process, placing the second crumpled sheet of plastic wrap beside the first, trying not to overlap the separate pieces. Continue until the whole sheet of paper—and out over the edges—is covered with the crumpled plastic. (See fig. 4–8.)

5 Let the plastic sit until the paint or ink dries; this will take a few hours. Then peel off the plastic to reveal the pattern. The pattern will be ruined if the plastic is removed before the paint or ink is dry. Rinse and reuse the plastic wrap, or discard it.

SAFETY WARNING ON SPRAY PAINTS

The next three techniques require spray paints, which raise health concerns. It is vital to work in a well-ventilated area because paint fumes can be harmful. People with respiratory problems should not use spray paint. Do not let students or children use spray paints unsupervised. Spread newspaper outdoors on the grass or indoors on a table in a well-ventilated room. Provide plenty of room for each person to work so that no one gets sprayed by mistake. These techniques are not safe for young children. Follow the manufacturer's instructions on the can of spray paint, and check the direction of the nozzle before beginning. Use a dust mask, and wear rubber gloves or apply a layer of barrier cream to protect your hands.

CRUMPLED AND SPRAYED PAPER

This technique uses spray paints to create a distinctive abstract pattern on paper. Though the paper is perfectly flat, it will look textured.

MATERIALS
- newspaper
- paper, commercial or handmade
- spray paints, two or three colors
- rubber gloves or *barrier cream* (heavy hand cream)
- dust mask
- steam iron and ironing board

DIRECTIONS

1 Cover the working space with newspaper. Gently crumple the paper into a ball. Use two hands, one on each side of the paper, pushing the paper with one hand into the palm of the other. This helps prevent ripping. Notice the even crumpling in fig. 4–9. If any parts of the paper are not crumpled, crumple them now. When crumpled evenly, open paper out just enough to lie flat.

2 Spray-painting crumpled paper is similar to the sun making shadows. When the sun is overhead, there are no shadows; in the late afternoon, the shadows are long and dramatic. To create dramatic color shadows, spray from a 20° angle. Start with light colors and work to darker colors. Spray across the crumpled paper from one side.

3 Turn the paper 90°, and spray with the second color. Turn the paper again and spray lightly with a third, darker color. The goal is to create a relatively even pattern of both sprayed and unsprayed areas. Let the paint dry for a few minutes.

4 Open the paper by pulling the opposite corners. Flatten it with your hands. If there are large spots with no paint, crumple new folds in those areas and spray lightly. The pattern should be a little uneven.

5 Let the paint dry for half an hour; then set the iron on medium. Lay your paper on the board and cover with plain scrap paper or fabric. Steam-iron the paper flat.

4–9 Create distinctive patterns by crumpling a large sheet of paper and spraying paint across it at a low angle. Try spraying different colors from different directions. Photo: E. Lancaster.

CREATIVE IDEAS

• Experiment with colored paper. Black or dark-green paper sprayed with bright gold paint is dramatic. Rust- or peach-colored paper sprayed with brown and gold paints gives an earthy feel. Use metallic spray paint, or mix warm and cool colors to add interest.

SPRAY-PAINTING WITH STENCILS

There are many items that you can use as stencils for spray-painting patterns on paper. Plant stencils create a natural look and are ideal for covering scrapbook or photograph albums. Other items to use are doilies, heavy lace, open-cut plastic placemats, loose-weave fabric remnants, buttons, and fly swatters; or commercial stencils and letter, circle, and French-curve templates. Because the stencil will be covered with paint, make sure that what you want to use is not valuable to anyone.

MATERIALS
• plant leaves
• newspaper
• spray paints, two colors
• paper, commercial or handmade
• rubber gloves or barrier cream
• dust mask

4–10 Make unique patterned papers by using the leaves of plants as stencils. These timeless-looking papers are ideal for book covers and endpapers, or on greeting cards. Photo: E. Lancaster.

DIRECTIONS

1 Choose your leaves (or other stencil); three or four leaves from the same plant work well together. If the leaves don't lie flat, press them under a book.

2 Cover the work surface with newspaper. Spray paint in one color at a time. Place the stencil flat on the paper. Spray lightly across it in one slow motion from about 8" (20 cm) away. Do not spray back and forth.

3 Move the stencil to other positions on the paper, spacing out the sprayed patterns in the first color. Change the stencil position each time so that the paper, when finished, can be viewed from any angle. Place and then spray the stencil partly off the edge of the paper to create the sense that the pattern continues.

4 Fill in any spaces by spraying the second color over the stencil. Add more of either color where needed. You can mix and match stencils.

4–11 Many common items can be used as stencils to create patterns with spray paints: lace, string, open-weave fabric, plastic placemats, old seat caning, metal washers, and letter templates. Photo: E. Lancaster.

CREATIVE IDEAS

• Combine gold and brown paint on white- or cream-colored papers for a classic look. Create a sense of depth by mixing light, dark, and midtone colors in your patterns.

• Use stencil paper or thin cardboard to make your own stencils. Because spray paints may corrode or dissolve some stencil films, test them first or use paper for the stencils you create.

5–1 Images are painted on recycled cotton fabric with wax, and are colored with vibrant dyes. Small rectangles of any decorated papers or fabric can be used to embellish the fronts of cards. Susan Schneider (United States), *Original Batik Cards,* 1995. Procion dyes, paraffin wax, cotton fabric, 5 x 7" (12.7 x 17.8 cm).

5–2 Dried leaves, fabric paint, wood-veneer strips, stamps, ribbon, and old maps are just some of the many items you can use to make collage cards. Three cards by Jean G. Kropper (Australia) 1995. Handmade and commercial papers, machine embroidery, found objects. Smallest: 3 1/2 x 2 3/4" (9 x 7 cm); largest: 4 1/2 x 6" (11.5 x 15.5 cm). Photo: E. Lancaster.

MAKING GREETING CARDS

Every culture commemorates historic events with yearly celebrations, and every religion has its holidays. What days are special to you? Do your friends celebrate traditions other than the ones you do? The special days celebrated throughout the world provide a rich diversity to life, and you can acknowledge any of these by making your own cards.

You can buy blank cards and envelopes in craft shops, art-supply stores, and stationery stores. Some cards have an embossed frame or a gold edge; some are plain; some are three-fold with a cut oval or rectangular window. You can get envelopes to match these cards, or you can make your own.

THE SIMPLEST CARDS

The simplest cards do not require any cutting or gluing, and you can make them in either a vertical or a horizontal format.

 ## VERTICAL CARDS

MATERIALS
- 8 1/2 x 11" (metric A4) sheet of paper
- bone folder

DIRECTIONS
Fold the sheet of paper along the width, matching the corners; and crease the fold with the bone folder. Fold and then crease the paper in half again, perpendicular to the first fold.

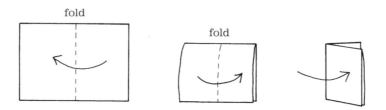

HORIZONTAL CARDS

DIRECTIONS

Fold the sheet of paper along the length, matching the corners; and crease the fold with the bone folder. Fold and then crease the paper in half again, perpendicular to the first fold.

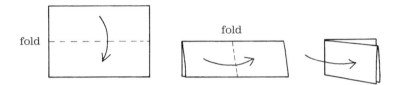

Decorate these blank cards any way you wish. Make a master in black and white and photocopy it, or make each one an original. Since you make these cards from text-weight paper, they are not very substantial, but they are easy to make and can suit many purposes.

BLANK CARDS

If you want blank cards in any size, color, or paper, you can make your own. You can make decisions about whether the cards will have a vertical or horizontal format, or whether they will have cut or torn edges. You can also make your own envelopes, or choose the envelopes first and then make the cards to fit them. Be sure that both length and width of your card is 3/8" (10 mm) smaller than the envelope. Select your colored paper at an art shop or from a printer. You may be able to buy leftover card stocks.

5–3 The artist was inspired by the mountains near his home in Waikato, New Zealand. The blue background is powdered pigment mixed with sizing; the mountain is blended pastel over white pulp painting; the black line is embossed, with black crayon added; and a linoleum print forms the pattern at the top. John Mitchell (New Zealand), *Mountain Card* (edition of 10), 1992. Handmade flax paper with pulp painting, thread, wood, pastel, and fixative, 8 11/16 x 9 7/16" (22 x 24 cm) when closed.

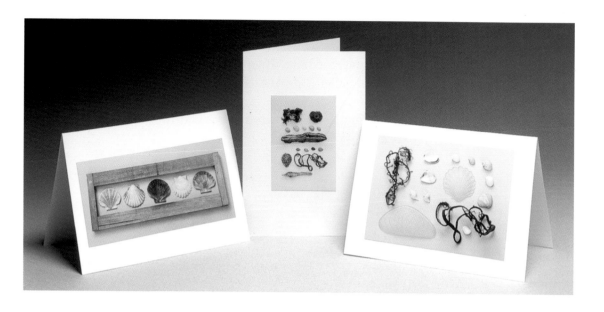

5–4 Sharp, colorful photographs so effectively capture shells, seaweed, and driftwood that you almost smell the sea. Agricultural waste from molasses production was used to make the paper for the cards. Lene Kuhl Jakobsen (Australia), *Once Upon a Beach*, 1994. Photographs, molasses paper, 6 x 4 5/16" (15.5 x 11 cm).

MATERIALS
- 50–90 lb (220–260 gsm) colored paper
- pencil
- triangle
- metal ruler
- craft knife with a new blade
- cutting mat
- bone folder

DIRECTIONS

1 Determine the grain direction of the paper. (See directions on page 22.) Using the triangle, metal ruler, craft knife, and cutting mat, mark with a pencil and then cut. (See pages 13–15.) Plan your cutting so that the folds will be parallel to the grain. When cutting a large sheet of paper, first cut it slightly larger than the size you want; then, in a second step, cut it exactly.

2 Measure the center and score the folds with the bone folder. Fold the paper in half at the scored lines and match the corners. Crease the paper by rubbing the bone folder diagonally over the paper from the open edges toward the fold.

SIMPLE DECORATIONS

You can create a matched set of cards both simply and inexpensively. Choose a photograph, wrapping paper, or fabric you like; or use your own patterned paper by following the directions in Chapter 4. You will cut rectangles of one of these items to decorate the front of your cards.

Make or buy blank cards and envelopes in the size you want. Measure the height and width of the front of the card. Subtract 3/4" (20 mm) from the height and width. Cut rectangles of the paper to this size. Working on newspaper, glue the back of these rectangles. Place them in the center on the front of the cards. Cover with scrap paper to protect your work, and burnish with the side of a bone folder.

FABRIC (OR DIMENSIONAL) PAINTS come in many colors—in tubes and in bottles—and are easy to use and fun to experiment with because the results are immediate. Keep the paint thin: in the mail, large globs on cards will squash flat; also, thinner dots and lines produce a better look. The paints may become slightly sticky in warm, humid weather, and should not be used on surfaces that will receive extensive handling. However, these paints are ideal for cards and stationery.

5-5 By using fabric (or dimensional) paint, you can decorate cards and stationery with colorful raised patterns. Photo: E. Lancaster.

Do some sketches on scrap paper; then draw the design on your paper and paint over the lines. Before beginning, shake the tube or bottle once, hard, to force paint down. Keep pressure steady as you squeeze to maintain an even line. To avoid smearing, let designs dry for twenty minutes.

MORE COMPLICATED CARDS

 ## THREE-FOLD CARDS

Although you can buy three-fold cards with a cut oval or rectangular window, you may want to make your own. You can make these cards in any color or dimension and in either format (horizontal or vertical). The three panels—A, B, and C—are shown in the diagram. Panels B and C are of equal width, but panel A is 1/16" (2 mm) narrower. (See *Windows*, fig. 10–19, on page 136.)

MATERIALS
- 60–130 lb (220–260 gsm) sheet of paper
- pencil
- triangle
- metal ruler
- craft knife and a new blade
- cutting mat
- bone folder
- glue stick or PVA glue and stencil brush

DIRECTIONS

1   Using the triangle, metal ruler, craft knife, and cutting mat, mark with a pencil and then cut the paper to the size you want. (See pages 13–15.) Then measure where to place the folds. Plan for panel A to be slightly narrower than panel B. Score with the bone folder.

2   On panel B, cut a window in the shape you want. To anchor the decoration in place, you will glue the decoration for your card to panel A, level with the window.

3   Use the glue stick or put a drop of PVA glue on the top left and bottom left of panel A. Fold panel A to the right; because it is slightly narrower, it should fit neatly on top of panel B. The decoration will be framed by the window.

4   Fold panels A and B together to the right, making sure that panel A is tucked in. Put the card under a weight for an hour while the glue dries.

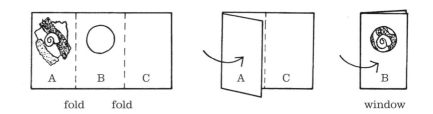

fold   fold   window

5–6 The windows in these commercially made three-fold cards reveal a colorful collage of handmade papers, woodcuts and etchings, gold threads and sequins. Judy Buist (Australia), *Planet Suite Cards,* 1995. Handmade papers, artist's woodcuts and etchings, gold threads, and sequins, 5 7/8 x 4 1/4" (15 x 10.8 cm) and 6 x 8" (15.2 x 20.3 cm).

5–7a, b This card, folded in the same manner as one unit of a star card, effectively combines type with the shape of the card. The numbers are cut from paper in a contrasting color and glued on one side only, popping up as the card is unfolded. Edward H. Hutchins, (United States), *Wilton's Birthday Gala,* 1995. When closed: 4 1/4" (10.8 cm) square; when open: 8 1/2" (21.6 cm) square. Photo: E. Lancaster.

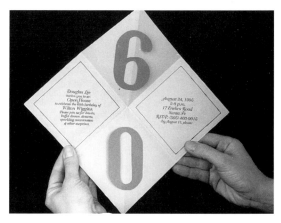

5–8 This card can either be folded to lie flat, or opened into a star shape, as shown. Attached ribbons tie the card open, which allows it to be hung as an ornament. Each unit in this star card is made of a different color of paper. Jane Wise-Gronewoller (United States), untitled, 1995. Hard covers and ribbon closing, 3 x 3 x 1 1/2" (7.6 x 7.6 x 3.8 cm), open; 1 1/4 x 1 1/4" (3.2 x 3.2 cm), closed.

 ## STAR CARDS

These cards can have messages on the inside, and may double as decorative ornaments. You can choose to make them large or small; of any color; with hard covers and ribbon closings; and from photocopy, construction, handmade, or decorative paper.

Knowing the direction of a fold will help you identify the correct side of the paper when following the steps of a project. A *mountain fold* is a fold that points up, like a mountain. A *valley fold* is a fold that points down, like a valley.

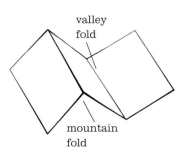

valley fold

mountain fold

MATERIALS
- 8 1/2 x 11" (metric A4) paper, 2 sheets
- pencil
- triangle
- metal ruler
- craft knife with a new blade
- cutting mat
- bone folder
- glue stick

MAKING THE BASIC UNITS

1 Using the triangle, metal ruler, craft knife, and cutting mat, mark with a pencil and then cut five equal squares of paper. (See pages 13–15.) Any size square is okay, but for your first attempt, cut four squares (4 1/4" or 10.5 cm per side) from one standard sheet of paper. Cut the fifth square from the other sheet of paper. Fold each square evenly in half, matching the corners.

2 Take one square and crease the fold, using your finger or a bone folder. If you are working with photocopy paper or another thin paper, you can crease the papers with your fingertip. You may, however, use the bone folder to achieve straighter folds. For straight folds on heavy paper, use the bone folder to score and then crease.

3 Unfold the paper. Follow the same procedure to fold in half in the other direction.

4 Unfold the square. Flip the square over and lay it flat on the table with the two folds pointing upwards in mountain folds.

5 Fold the sheet diagonally once, corner to corner, across the mountain folds.

6 Crease the fold. Leave it folded (it will be triangular).

7 Lift up the folded sheet with two hands with the open end of each triangle pointing away from you. Place your thumbs along the diagonal fold near the center. Press with both thumbs at the same time.

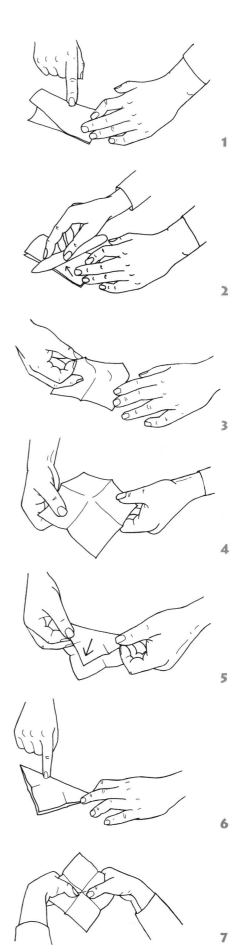

5–9 The symmetrical pattern of a sky-scraper is achieved in this side-by-side card by making cuts to an assembled card that is folded up and laid flat. Sally Read (Australia), *City Buildings,* 1995. 2 3/4 x 5 1/2 x 2" (7 x 14 x 5 cm), open.

CREATIVE IDEAS

• For side-by-side units, cut the shape of the open end of each unit to change the shape of the card. Cut rounded or scalloped shapes (to look like petals); or for a lacy effect when the card is open, cut triangular notches through all the layers. With the card closed and laid flat on a cutting mat, cut the card after you have glued all the units together.

You can cut notches and do limited cutting on alternating-unit cards. However, if you cut into the connecting folds too much, the structure becomes weakened.

• Alternate the color of the units in a card, or glue two papers back to back to create squares with different colors on either side.

• Cut square images or parts of images from your own artwork or from pictures in magazines or newspapers. Use a glue stick to back these with plain paper; then make them into side-by-side cards. Leave one unit (or more) plain where you want to write messages. You can also add images to alternating-unit cards, but parts of them will be covered where the units interlock.

5–10 Any decorated papers can be cut into rectangles to decorate a set of cards. Try marbled paper, gift wrap, old maps, sections of magazine photos, or (shown here) paste papers made by the artist. Peggy Skycraft (United States), 1995. 4 1/2 x 6 1/4" (11.4 x 15.8 cm) and 6 1/4 x 4 1/2".

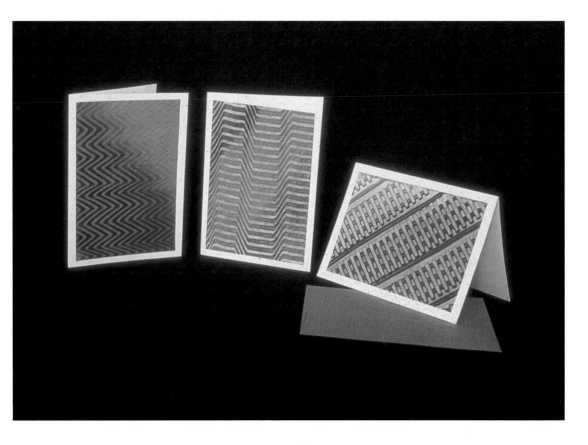

ENVELOPES

Make matching envelopes for your cards with handmade or commercial paper. If you plan to mail the card, make the envelope a standard size and out of sturdy paper. Oversized envelopes often require extra postage.

To make an envelope easily, find a ready-made envelope of the size you want. Open it out flat and use it as a template to trace in pencil onto the paper you have chosen. Cut out the shape with scissors, score and crease the folds, and then glue with a glue stick where necessary (look at the original envelope). Put your finished card into the envelope, and seal it with glue.

5–11a, b Make your own envelopes by cutting them from unusual papers, photographs in magazines, or maps. Use an old envelope opened out flat as a template. Trace around it, then cut, fold, and glue it to match your sample.

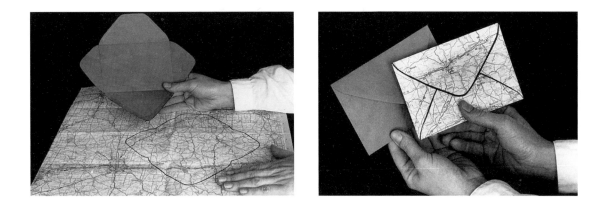

6

6–1 A fascination with the power of myths inspired these blank books made with fabric collage, plastic gems, old coins, yarn, and fish- and bird-shaped beads. Jean G. Kropper (Australia), *Journal for a Sea Voyage* (left), 1995. Recycled handmade paper covers with plant fiber and Coptic binding, 12 x 8 x 1" (30.5 x 20.3 x 2.54 cm). *Journal for a Wandering Mind* (right), 1995. Cover made with dyed wild ginger plant fiber paper, with a variation of Japanese stab binding, 13 x 9 1/2 x 1" (33 x 24.1 x 2.54 cm).

6–2 Two copies of this limited-edition book display its Japanese stab binding from the outside (right) and a transparent flyleaf inside (left). The book combines quotations from Jack Kerouac with commentary photos. Susan Kapuscinski Gaylord (United States), *Contradictions*, 1990. Calligraphy on tracing vellum; photos manipulated on a photocopier, 5 5/8 x 8 5/8" (14.3 x 21.9 cm).

DESIGNING BOOKS: GETTING STARTED

It is easier to make choices about designing books when you have the vocabulary to specifically describe what you want. Here are some terms you will need to know.

BOOKBINDING TERMS

LEAF A flat sheet of paper in its entirety, or both sides of a sheet of paper.

PAGE One side of a leaf, or a sheet of paper that has writing on it.

FOLIO OR FOLD A single sheet of paper that has been folded in half. This becomes two leaves, or four pages or sides.

SECTION OR SIGNATURE A group of folded sheets, or folios, bound as a unit.

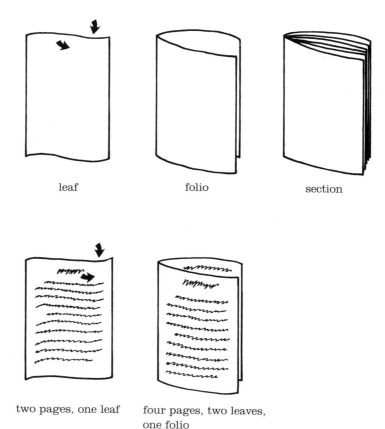

leaf   folio   section

two pages, one leaf   four pages, two leaves, one folio

BOARDS The generic term for the cardboard, greyboard, archivite, or other material used for the hard covers of a book.

ENDPAPERS The paper pasted onto the inside of the front and back covers of a hardcover book. They form a visual transition from the outside to the inside of the book. All the bindings shown in this book have *single* endpapers. However, a multisection case-bound (hardcover) book, like this one, has *double* endpapers. An endpaper is pasted to the inside of each cover (like single endpapers) and then continues across the crease and becomes the first (and last) free leaf between the covers and the text. Endpapers are often colored or decorated, but are not given page numbers.

FLYLEAF or **FLYSHEET** An optional first leaf or page before the text pages. It may or may not have text, and sometimes is translucent (like tracing paper).

FORE EDGE The side of the book that opens; the side opposite the spine. In a Western codex book, it is the right edge.

HEAD The top or upper horizontal edge of a book or page.

SQUARE The amount a cover extends beyond the text pages in a book. Japanese stab, concertina, and Coptic-bound books have squares that are 1/16" (1.5 mm) or less. A hardcover album may have 1/4" (6 mm) squares.

TAIL The bottom or lower horizontal edge of a book or page.

SPINE The edge of the book where the pages are bound together. In a typical Western codex book, it is the left side. *Spine* also refers to the part of the cover along this bound, or closed, side.

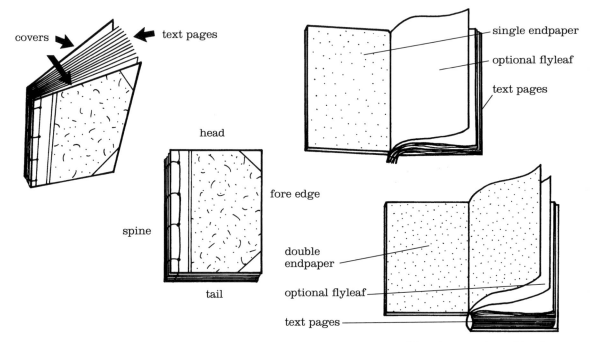

multisection case-bound book

TEXT PAGES OR TEXT BLOCK The pages between the covers. They form the bulk of the book and may contain text and/or images.

SOFT COVERS Covers made from text-weight (light) or cover-weight (heavy) paper, flexible enough to bend without cracking, and forming their own *hinge* when folded.

HARD COVERS Often wrapped on the outside with *cover paper* and on the inside with endpapers, these covers are made from rigid cardboard (boards)—or from wood, Plexiglas™, or metal. Since the covers themselves cannot bend, they must hinge from the side or have a paper hinge added.

AN OVERVIEW OF BINDINGS

PAMPHLET BINDINGS are simple bindings for one section of folded sheets (or folios). They have a soft cover and lie flat when open. *Quick and easy.*

JAPANESE STAB BINDINGS hold single sheets of paper (leaves) in a soft cover. Pages do not lie flat when open. *Quick and easy.*

HARDCOVER ALBUMS hold single sheets of paper (leaves) in a hard cover. You can unbind, add, or subtract pages, and then rebind the album fairly easily. These are ideal for scrapbooks, photo albums, and visitor's books. Pages do not lie flat when open. *Medium difficulty; a few hours to complete.*

CROSSED-RIBBON BINDINGS are suitable for softcover or hardcover books, especially wedding and photo albums. Pages do not lie flat when open. *Quick and easy on softcovers; medium difficulty on hardcovers.*

pamphlet binding

hardcover album

Japanese stab binding

crossed-ribbon binding

CONCERTINA BINDINGS are formed in a continuous length of paper with zigzag folds. There is no sewing in this kind of binding, also called *accordion* or *leporello* binding. The variations of this binding are described below. *Easy to medium difficulty.*

• Simple concertinas can be opened flat for viewing all the pages at once, making these well suited to panoramic paintings and long messages. This binding automatically expands to fit items—such as pressed flowers or artwork—that you wish to add. *Easy to medium difficulty.*

• Continuous concertinas suit books with mostly images and little text. The first and last pages of a simple concertina are connected to form the continuous loop. *Quick and easy.*

• Concertina spine bindings with inserted pages require a narrow concertina for the spine only. Each page is a separate piece of paper (or leaf) glued (or pasted) into the concertina. Made with a hard or soft cover, this form is ideal for displaying both sides of each page. These books lie flat when open to any page, since the pages hinge from the binding. *Medium difficulty.*

• Concertina spine bindings with pamphlets sewn in require a narrow concertina for the spine only. Made with a hard or soft cover, this form is ideal for holding letters or greeting cards, which are sewn into the narrow concertina. *Medium difficulty; a few hours to bind.*

COPTIC BINDINGS have several sections or groups of folios and are made with a hard or soft cover. The binding is left exposed on the spine. The pages open flat, making them ideal for diaries, address books, or a collection of newsletters. This binding is quite complicated and is not for the beginner. *High difficulty; a few hours to complete.*

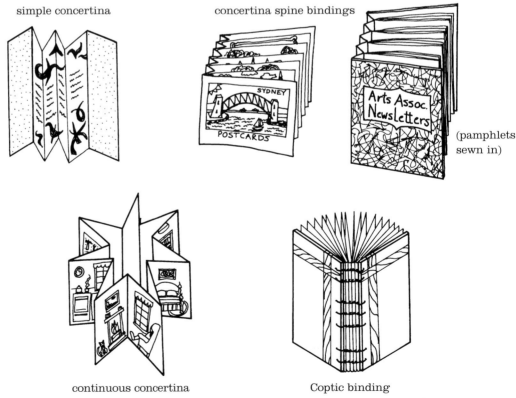

simple concertina   concertina spine bindings

(pamphlets sewn in)

continuous concertina   Coptic binding

What is your definition of a book? Must it have type, images, covers, and paper pages? Before you make a hand-bound book, you need to clarify what sort of book it will be, how it will be used, and who will use it. This will help you choose the appropriate design and binding technique. Write your answers to the following questions; leave those you are unsure about, and come back to them later.

6-3 The design of this book reflects the author's message— the power of dreams to transcend borders. Genie Shenk (United States), *Crossing Borders,* 1993. Horizontal format concertina book with digital type, photocopied paper, 2 1/2 x 36" (6.4 x 91.4 cm).

 ## THE BASICS

•   What is the book's purpose? Will the book hold a written story, images, or both? Who will use the book?

•   What shape will the book have? Rectangular? Sculptural? Will it have a horizontal or a vertical format?

•   Will the book be bound on the left side, the right side, or across the top?

•   How many pages are needed? Will they be divided into chapters or sections?

•   What size will the book be? Does it need to be large enough to hold photo enlargements or newspaper articles?

•   Will the book have a hard or a soft cover? Should it be durable enough for young children to use?

•   What colors for the cover and the text will best suit the message?

•   What kind of paper is right for the cover and the text pages? Textured, smooth, lined, dark, light, opaque, translucent, handmade, commercially made, acid-free?

•   Will the book have set content or open content? (See pages 62–63.)

•   Will the book be a single copy, or an edition of books that are all the same?

6–4 A twelve-page simple concertina book (called a *leporello* in Europe) with hard covers. Helga Schröder (Germany), *Book LX: Christa Wolf—Was nicht in den tage-büchern steht* (Words not kept in a diary), 1995. Lithography, collage, and drawing on Hahnemuhle paper, 14 x 9 7/8" (35 x 25 cm). Printed at the Janus Press, Berlin.

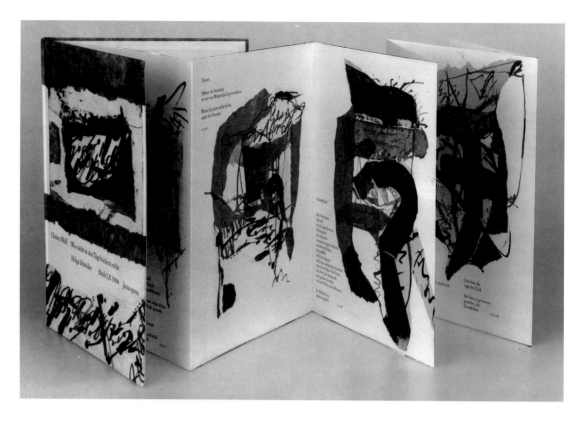

 ## SET CONTENT

If you have a story, poem, or series of images that you have decided to put into book form, you have set content for the book. For a *set-content* book, answer these questions.

• How much text is there? How will you divide it among the pages?

• What typeface will you use? How large do you want the type? Do you have access to word-processing software and a printer?

• Do you want any illustrations or photos to go with the text? If so, will they be in black and white or in color?

• If you are producing more than one copy, how will the book be reproduced?

• Will the text be on single leaves or on folios? How much of a margin or gutter (space between columns of type) will you need for the binding? Read on, and then come back to answer the remaining questions.

OPEN CONTENT

If you have chosen the kind of material to put into a book but not the material itself, you have *open content* for the book. You add the content after you have made the book. Photo albums, diaries, and scrapbooks are open-content books. For an open-content book, answer these questions.

• Will items be glued into the book at a later date? (If so, the thickness of these items must be allowed for in the binding.)

• Is the book to be written in after binding? (If so, the paper must be smooth enough for writing.)

• Start with a short story about your family (an example of set content). If you have access to a computer, make a printout of your family's name and glue it to the front cover. Put a photograph of your family on the title page. Type the story on 8 1/2 x 11" (metric A4) paper, leaving a wide left margin; bind the pages with a Japanese stab binding. (See page 68.)

• From a panoramic drawing of a landscape, make a concertina book with separate hard covers. (See Chapter 8.) Open the book for display.

• Write a poem in delicate calligraphy on folios small enough to fit into a pocket. Bind them with the *pamphlet stitch* (see page 64), and make a watercolor painting for the cover.

• Create a wedding-photo album with white or cream acid-free pages large enough to fit two 5 x 7" (12.7 x 17.8 cm) photographs side by side. Write captions in gold ink. Use acid-free glue and acid-free cardboard for the boards, and bind the album in a hard cover. (See Chapter 7.)

• Print a collection of recipes onto colored pages of different shapes. Use one shape for a section of appetizer recipes, another for a section of main-dish recipes, and so on. (See "Shaped Pages" on page 129.) For the front cover, make a collage of pictures from magazines. Bind with a hard or soft cover with a crossed-ribbon binding. (See page 72.)

• Make a class book (see page 34) of ideas for cleaning up the environment. Have participants make one page each and all the members plan and decorate a soft cover with spray-painted plant stencils (see page 42). Use recycled-paper pages and either a Japanese stab or crossed-ribbon binding.

• Use a concertina binding with soft covers to hold (page 96) a collection of birthday or holiday cards and bind them with pamphlet stitch. Make the covers slightly larger than the largest card.

6–5 Dedicated to the artist's mother after her death, these pamphlet-bound books contain four short, rather somber poems by Percy Bysshe Shelley. Stephanie Later (United States), *Four by Shelley*, 1992. Letterpress-printed poems, hand-illustrated, wooden covers with sculptured texture, 4 1/2 x 21 1/2 x 1 1/2" (11.4 x 54.6 x 3.8 cm).

6–6 The tassels binding this single-section pamphlet are decorated with fish bones, worn glass, corroded metal scraps, and shells. Some objects are also collaged on pages behind a cutout window; other pages are left blank for sketching and creative writing. Gladys Dove (Western Australia), *Seashore Collection,* 1995. Handmade paper made by the artist from cotton linter, kozo, and abaca fiber, 6 1/4 x 4 7/8 x 5/8" (15.8 x 12.4 x 1.5 cm).

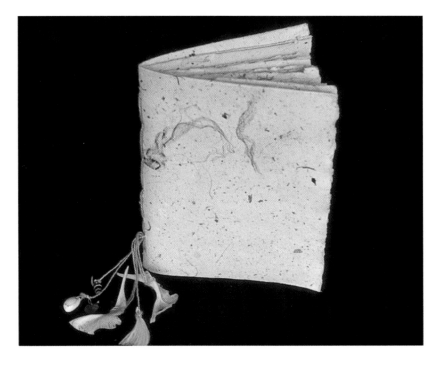

SIMPLE BINDING TECHNIQUES

You can choose among many ways to bind pages together into a book, and then make variations to the bindings presented here.

PAMPHLET BINDING

This is one of the simplest ways to bind sheets of paper. Many magazines and newsletters are pamphlet-bound, although magazines are stapled instead of sewn. This technique is especially suitable for both young children and beginners.

MATERIALS
- 10–20 sheets of text paper
- 70–120 lb (140–240 gsm) cover paper, patterned or plain
- pencil
- triangle
- metal ruler
- craft knife with a new blade
- cutting mat
- bone folder
- darning or tapestry needle
- linen or embroidery thread
- awl or compass point
- scissors

PREPARING TO BIND

1   Start with ten uniformly-sized sheets of paper, plus one sheet for a template. Find the grain direction. In groups of five sheets, loosely fold the papers in half, parallel to the grain, matching up the corners. Hold the corners with one hand, and slide the bone folder diagonally from the open edges toward the fold to crease the paper, creating a folio (see page 14, illustration 2). Pamphlet books are made of one section, or several folios folded inside each other.

2 The covers for this pamphlet book are soft. Check the grain direction of the cover paper, and plan which way to cut it. Using the triangle, metal ruler, craft knife, and cutting mat, mark with a pencil and then cut the cover 1/8" (3 mm) taller and wider than the text pages. If your book has more than ten folios, make the cover 1/8" (3 mm) taller and 1/4" (6 mm) wider than the text pages (or trim the pages along the fore edge after binding to make them even). Measure and mark where the crease is to be, score the crease, and fold the cover paper in half. Place the cover around the text pages.

3 Take out the extra folio; it is your template for piercing holes for binding. Open this template flat on the work surface. Measure vertically along the crease to find the center, and mark this with a needle hole. From this point, measure up 2" (50 mm) and down 2" (50 mm) and mark these spots with a needle hole. These measurements may be less if your book is small.

If your book is tall, or needs a five-hole binding because it has a lot of pages, measure up and down another 2–2 1/2" (50–62 mm) from these holes. Again, mark the places with needle holes. This template can be reused for other pamphlet-bound books with the same spine height.

4 Place your template inside the other folios. Wrap the cover around the outside. Tap the pages against the spine and against the head, or the top of the pages, to align them. Place them to one side of the work surface.

5 Hold an awl, compass point, or large sharp needle in your writing hand. With your other hand, open out the pages to form a 90°, or right, angle. Pierce the pages at the places marked on the template page, by going through the sheets at a 45° angle. The 45° angle is important; otherwise, the hole is pierced at different points in relation to the crease for different folios. Take your time and watch where the needle is in relation to your fingers.

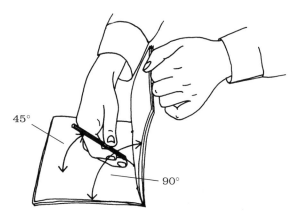

6 Check that the folios are lined up properly. Tap them against the spine and the head.

BINDING A THREE-HOLE PAMPHLET

1 Cut a length of thread twice the height of the book, and thread the needle. Begin sewing by entering the middle hole from the inside of the book, pushing the needle through the holes already pierced; do not create new holes. Pull the needle through to the outside of the book, leaving 2" (50 mm) of thread inside. Enter the lowest hole from the outside of the spine, pushing the needle through the holes to the inside. Pull the needle until the thread is tight. (Except for leaving the beginning tail of thread, always pull the thread tight, parallel to the spine in the direction you are working.) Go up to the top hole.

2 Enter the top hole from the inside of the book. Work through existing holes; do not create new ones. Pull the thread tight. Enter the middle hole from the outside of the spine, and poke the tip of the needle through to one side of the thread already there.

3 Once you have poked through to the inside, pause. Look inside. Notice that the beginning tail of the thread is to one side of the vertical stitch that passes over this hole. Come through on the *other* side of this stitch. Gently pull the thread tight, and remove the needle. Tie the two ends of the thread together in a *square knot* (see the glossary, page 142) across the stitch. Cut the threads 1/4" (6 mm) from the knot. You have completed your first book!

BINDING A FIVE-HOLE PAMPHLET

The design and preparation of the covers and text pages for a five-hole pamphlet is the same as for a three-hole pamphlet. The binding is done similarly, but there is one extra stitch at the head and at the tail. If you are making extra-tall books, add two stitches at the head and two at the tail.

1 Cut a length of thread twice the height of the book, and thread the needle. Enter the center hole from the inside of the book, as with a three-hole pamphlet. Pull the needle through to the outside, leaving 2" (50 mm) of thread inside. Enter the next hole below this point, from the outside of the spine. Push the needle through to the inside, and pull gently toward the tail of the book, the direction you will be going next. Pull until the thread is tight. Next, enter the lowest hole (at the tail) from the inside, and pull the thread through to the outside of the spine.

2 Enter the second hole up from the outside of the spine, and come through to the inside. Pull gently until the thread is tight. Skip over the center hole, enter the second hole from the top from the inside, and go through to the outside. Go up to the top hole, entering it from the outside to the inside. Pull the thread tight.

3 Enter the second hole from the top from the inside, and go through to the outside. Enter the middle hole from the outside of the spine, and poke the tip of the needle through to one side of the thread already there.

4 Once you have poked through to the inside, pause. Look inside. Notice that the beginning tail of the thread is to one side of the vertical stitch that passes over this hole. Come through on the *other* side of this stitch. Gently pull the thread tight, and remove the needle. Tie the two ends of the thread together in a square knot over the vertical stitch. Cut the thread end 1/4" (7 mm) from the knot. You are done!

CREATIVE IDEAS

• Add a distinctive touch to pamphlet-bound books by stringing beads on the sewing thread on the outside of the binding. Do not add beads to the inside of the binding because they will rub against the papers and cause wear. Beads can also be added on the outside of Japanese stab or Coptic bindings. (See fig. 6-1 and fig. 6-7 for examples.)

If you start and end the binding on the outside of the book, leave the beginning and ending threads long, and string them with beads.

• Instead of folding your paper evenly in half, matching the corners, fold it to one side of the center, or at an angle across the center. This gives different shapes to the pages—and to the whole book. Alternating differently colored pages will accentuate the effect.

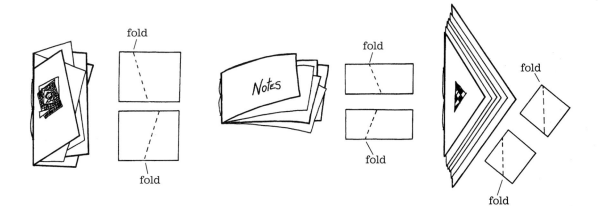

JAPANESE STAB BINDING

This technique is ideal for binding single sheets of paper in soft covers and can be used for diaries, class notes, phone messages, recipes, and school or business reports.

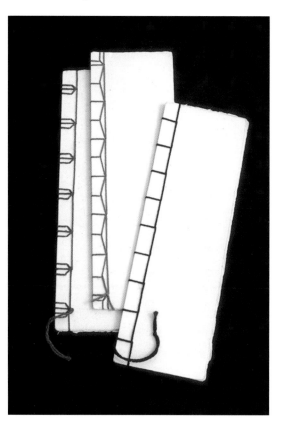

6–7 These Japanese stab books are bound with colored embroidery thread in three different variations of the binding, each with its own name: the tortoise shell binding (left), the hemp leaf binding (center), and the traditional stab binding (right). Made from Fabriano printmaking paper for use as teaching samples. Adèle Outteridge (Australia), 1993. 11 1/4 x 3 3/4 x 1/4" (28.6 x 9.5 x 5 cm).

Most types of papers—handmade, commercial or tracing papers, even acetate —can be used for Japanese stab binding. If the book will contain writing, the paper must be smooth. Inexpensive photocopy paper is also fine for text pages, and has the added benefit of being readily available and cut to a standard size. Cutting is not required for this technique, which makes it suitable for both young and beginner bookbinders.

Although the cover for this binding is always soft, it can be single sheets of heavy card-weight paper, single sheets with a turned-in flap, or sheets doubled over. The cover also can be one piece that wraps around the spine to give the pages more protection.

MATERIALS
- 20–50 sheets of text paper, cut to the same size
- 70–100 lb (140–200 gsm) paper, for the front and back covers
- pencil
- triangle
- metal ruler
- craft knife with a new blade
- cutting mat
- leather hole punch, 1/16 to 1/8" (1 to 3 mm)—or electric drill and fine drill bit—and a small hammer (**Note:** the size of the holes depends on the thickness of the thread or yarn used for binding.)
- binding thread
- darning or tapestry needle
- scissors

PREPARING TO BIND

1 Choose your cover option and the paper for the text pages. Based on its intended use and the paper available, decide the size of your book and the number of pages.

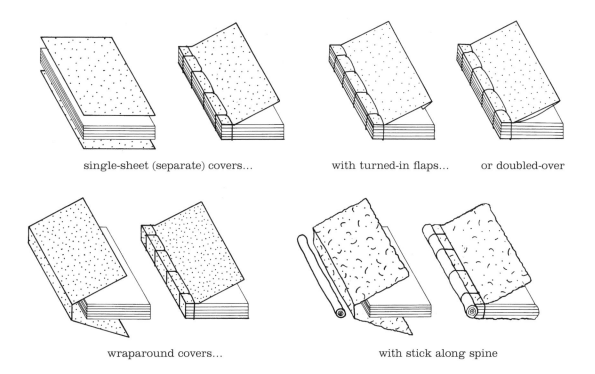

single-sheet (separate) covers...   with turned-in flaps...   or doubled-over

wraparound covers...   with stick along spine

template for
piercing holes

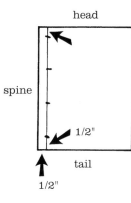

2   Using the triangle, metal ruler, craft knife, and cutting mat, mark with a pencil and then cut all text pages to size, or start with paper cut to a standard size, such as 8 1/2 x 11" (metric A4). (See page 13–15.) Then cut two pieces of scrap paper to the same size as the text pages, reserving one for a template and the other to place underneath the text pages to protect them during handling.

3   Using the triangle, ruler, and pencil, measure 1/2" (12 mm) from the left side of the template and draw a straight line. Measure 1/2" (12 mm) down from the head and 1/2" (12 mm) up from the tail, and mark these points on the line. These will be the lowest and highest sewing holes (*sewing stations*).

Measure the distance between these marks along the line. Divide that distance into equal parts and mark two other points along the line. These four marks on the template show where to punch holes. Four-hole binding is traditional, though five or more holes may be used.

6–8 A leather hole punch is used on this stack of text pages for a Japanese stab or an album binding. A simple template marks the position of the holes. Photo: E. Lancaster.

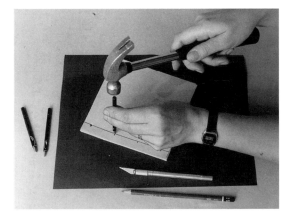

4   Line up the text pages, and place them on thick cardboard or a wood board, not on a self-sealing cutting mat, which would become permanently damaged. Put the template on top of the text pages. Punch the holes with the leather hole punch and a small hammer, or with an electric drill.

With the leather hole punch, punch only twenty pages at a time. If you punch more, the pages—and the holes—will slip out of alignment. Use the template to mark the position of the holes for each lot of twenty pages. Check that each hole goes through all the pages.

In a classroom situation, the teacher can show two students or aides how to punch the holes; they then help everyone else with this step.

If you use a drill, place all the pages between two pieces of wood, with the top board just back from where the holes will be drilled. Place this sandwich on the edge of a bench or table and tighten a C-clamp around it and the bench; if you have two C-clamps, use one on either end. This will hold the pages in place while you drill. *If you are unfamiliar with power tools, ask someone who is familiar with them to help. Power tools can be dangerous if you do not know how to handle them.*

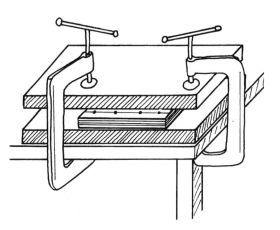

5 Cut the cover paper 1/16" (2 mm) larger (both length and width) than the text pages. There is no overhang—or *square*—on covers with this binding; the covers are the same size or only a fraction larger than the text pages. Using the template, punch holes in the covers. Assemble the text pages, and put the covers in position.

BINDING IT TOGETHER

1 Cut a length of thread four times the height of the binding, and thread the needle. Hold the covers and the text pages together, and enter the lowest hole on the front cover, going through to the back. Pull the needle and thread through, leaving 2" (50 mm) of thread at the tail of the book. Thread around the tail, and through the same hole from the front cover. Thread around the spine and through the same hole again, coming out the back. Enter the next hole up from the back, and come out the front of the book.

2 Thread around the spine, and enter the same hole again from the back, coming out the front. Enter the next hole from front to back. Thread around the spine, and enter the same hole again from front to back. Go up to the next, or top, hole, and enter from back to front.

3 Thread around the spine and enter the same hole from the back, coming out the front. Thread around the head, and enter the same hole from the back. Your needle should be on the front, having just come out of the top hole. Go into the second hole down from front to back. On the back, go into the third hole down from back to front.

4 Move to the lowest hole, and remove the needle. Tie a square knot directly over the hole, leaving the tail of the thread. Cut the threads 1/4" (6 mm) away from the knot. Use the needle to tuck the ends into the hole.

HARDCOVER ALBUMS

A hardcover album can hold a variety of items, including memorabilia from a trip overseas, a series of sketches or watercolors, newspaper clippings, a class or business presentation, or photos. It holds single leaves of paper in a hard cover. Hardcover albums are essentially Japanese stab books with a hard cover, and they have the same advantages.

Most papers can be used, but heavy 80 lb (160 gsm) opaque colored paper is ideal for the cover and inside pages. The papers can be in bright or pale colors, commercial or handmade, lined or blank, and may have a slightly textured surface. However, if the book is to be written in, the paper must be smooth. Endpapers can be made from the same paper in a different color or from decorated papers.

INSIDE THE ALBUM

CONCEPT AND DESIGN

Design your album to fit the character of what it will contain. Refer to the questions on pages 61–62, and think about what you want your album to look like. See Chapter 10 for design ideas. Paper, PVA glue, and boards—all acid-free—are necessary for any book you want to keep for a long time. (See page 23.) If you want shaped pages, windows, machine embroidery, or any other decoration, add them now.

PREPARING THE TEXT PAGES

You will cut large sheets of paper into four leaves for text pages. If you want to make a scrapbook, photo album, or any other book in which you will glue items, you will need *guards*, extra folds of paper added to the edge of a page to allow for the thickness of items glued onto the pages later. Without guards, the binding will eventually weaken or break. You will not need guards if nothing will be glued into the book.

MATERIALS
- 80 lb (160 gsm) opaque paper, 22 x 30" (55 x 75 cm), several sheets
- pencil
- triangle
- metal ruler
- craft knife with a new blade
- cutting mat
- bone folder
- scissors

End view of album bindings.

no items glued in
(no guards)

no items glued in
(with guards)

items glued in
(no guards)

items glued in
(with guards)

single page with a
guard folded over 1"

DIRECTIONS

1 Find the paper's grain direction; it is usually parallel to the shorter side (see page 22). Using the triangle, metal ruler, craft knife, and cutting mat, mark with a pencil and then cut the paper with the grain parallel to the spine. (See pages 13–15.) When the sheets of paper are cut in half in both directions, you will have four horizontal pages, 11 x 15" (27.5 x 37.5 cm), each large enough to hold four standard-size photos horizontally, or one 8 1/2 x 11" (metric A4). **Note:** Because the album will not open flat, leave a 1 1/4" (31 mm) margin down the binding side of each page, where nothing will be written or glued, regardless of the book's use.

Cut as many pages as you need, keeping two full-size sheets of paper for the cover. Stack the pages on top of each other, and check that their sizes match. Trim them if needed.

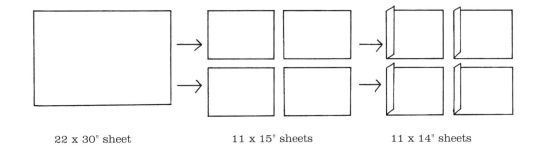

22 x 30" sheet   11 x 15" sheets   11 x 14" sheets

2 For each page, measure and mark in three places 1" (25 mm) from the short edge. Line up the ruler with the marks, and score from top to bottom with the bone folder. Fold the 1" (25 mm) flap, or guard, and crease it with the bone folder. Fold each guard onto the front of its own page, not around any other pages. Each page now measures 11 x 14" (27.5 x 35 cm). **Note:** If you do not need guards, you can either cut 1" (25 mm) off the side of each leaf, keeping all other sides the same, or you can keep the leaves as they are and make the covers, cover paper, and endpapers 1" (25 mm) wider. Stack the pages in the correct order.

MAKING HARD COVERS

The basic steps for making hard covers include cutting cardboard 1/4–1/2" (6–12 mm) larger than the text pages, cutting these boards in two, and adding paper hinges. These are then wrapped on the outside with cover paper and on the inside with endpapers. Holes are punched, and the covers and text pages are bound together.

7–2 A linocut image, inspired by a Japanese Samurai sword guard, is inset into the cover of this hardcover album. Bound with conso chord (used by jewelers) and silver beads, the book is designed to hold photos and memorabilia. Debra Glanz (United States), *Album with Linocut,* 1993. Bookcloth binding with an inset linocut print; text pages are Stonehenge paper with silver beads added to the binding, 8 x 9" (20.3 x 22.9 cm).

MATERIALS
- 1/8" (2–3 mm) thick cardboard (greyboard or archivite) (**Note:** Always use solid, not corrugated, cardboard. Use acid-free board and PVA glue if your text pages are acid-free.)
- 1 sheet 8 1/2 x 11" (metric A4) paper, for hinges: any fine Japanese paper, such as kozo (mulberry paper); abaca (manila hemp); or your chosen cover paper
- pencil
- triangle
- metal ruler
- craft knife with a new blade
- cutting mat
- newspaper
- PVA glue and stencil brush
- nonstick paper
- bone folder

DIRECTIONS

1 Find the cardboard's grain direction; plan your cutting so that the grain will be parallel to the spine. Finding the grain direction in cardboard is the same as for paper: you can tear it or bounce it. (See page 22.)

Using the triangle, metal ruler, craft knife, and cutting mat, mark with a pencil and then cut the cover boards to 11 1/2 x 14 1/4" (29.2 x 36.2 cm). Albums have larger squares (the amount the covers overhang the text pages) than books previously described. This follows the general guideline that covers are 1/4" to 1/2" larger than the text pages. Trim the boards so that they match exactly.

Along one of the short 11 1/2" (29.2 cm) sides, measure in 1" (25 mm) in three places and mark these points with a pencil. Draw a vertical line through these points; then cut the cover boards. The gap left between this strip and the rest of the cover board will form a hinge.

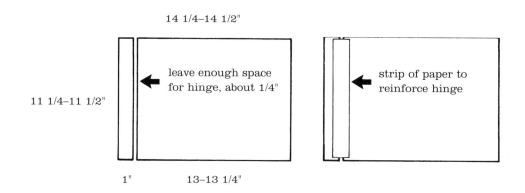

14 1/4–14 1/2"

11 1/4–11 1/2"

leave enough space for hinge, about 1/4"

strip of paper to reinforce hinge

1"   13–13 1/4"

2   Cut two strips of your selected paper for hinges: 1–1 1/4" (25–30 mm) wide and 11 1/4" (28.6 cm) long. You will glue these strips across the gap between the two parts of both cover boards, forming a hinge. This will set the width of the hinge and reinforce it, but later will be hidden by the cover paper. Cover the work surface with newspaper, and lay down the strips side by side. Dab a stencil brush into PVA glue, and pound the brush vertically onto these strips. Let the glue become tacky—for five to ten minutes—while proceeding with the next step.

3   Now decide how wide the hinge will be. Look closely at how the hinge sits when the cover is open, wrapping around the edges of the two parts of the cover board.

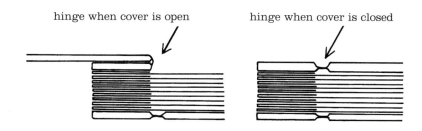

hinge when cover is open   hinge when cover is closed

Measure the thickness of the cardboard you chose for the covers. The width of the hinge should be two times the thickness of the cover boards, plus another 1/16" (2.5 mm). Check your measurements carefully; you do not want to make the hinges too narrow, because the covers will not open flat. Lay out the cover boards and glued strips flat on clean newspaper. Adjust the space between the cover boards and strips to the width you choose.

4   Center one paper strip, glue side down, over the gap for the hinge on one of the covers. (The strip will have one edge on each of the two parts of the cover board). Cover with nonstick paper, and burnish with the side of the bone folder to ensure that the paper adheres to the boards. Repeat this step with the second strip on the other cover. Replace any used newspaper on the work surface.

5   Recheck the cover dimensions. Sometimes, adding the hinges makes the covers wider than expected, and you may need to trim 1/8" (3 mm) off the fore edge. The covers should be 1/4–1/2" (6–12 mm) larger in both width and length than the text pages (not counting the guard).

WRAPPING THE BOARDS WITH COVER PAPER

MATERIALS

- 80 lb (160 gsm) opaque colored paper, 22 x 30" (56 x 76 cm), several full-size sheets, for the covers
- pencil
- triangle
- metal ruler
- craft knife with a new blade
- cutting mat
- newspaper
- nonstick paper
- book press or 2 C-clamps and 2 pressing boards (see page 21)
- spring-loaded divider or compass
- scissors
- fine sandpaper (optional)

DIRECTIONS

1   Using the triangle, metal ruler, craft knife, and cutting mat, mark with a pencil and then cut two pieces of cover paper, either decorated or plain, 2" (50 mm) larger in both width and length than your cover boards, or about 13 1/2 x 16 1/2" (33.7 x 41.2 cm), with the grain parallel to the spine. (See pages 13–15.) These dimensions allow 1" (25 mm) all around for wrapping around the edges of the cover boards. Lay out the papers wrong side up. Center the cover boards on the paper, and trace their position lightly in pencil. Put aside the cover paper, wrong side up, on a clean surface.

2   Lay out the two boards on clean newspaper. (The strips you glued earlier should be facedown.) Apply PVA with a stencil brush, pounding the glue onto the cardboard. Leave for five to ten minutes for the glue to become tacky.

3   Place the cover boards on the cover paper, glue side down, inside the traced marks. (The glued-on strips should now be facing up.) Put a sheet of nonstick paper on top, and burnish the boards onto the cover paper to help it adhere and to work out any air bubbles. Flip the covers over placing them on clean newspaper, put the nonstick paper on top, and burnish again. Flip the cover over a second time so that the cover paper is on the underside.

4   The next step is to cut the corners of the cover paper at a 45° angle, leaving just enough paper to wrap neatly around the cover boards. The amount of paper you should leave depends on the thickness of the cardboard you have used for the covers. Measure the thickness of the cardboard, usually about 1/8" (2–3 mm), and multiply by 1 1/2 or 2. Mark this distance in pencil, measuring diagonally out from the corners of the cover boards on the back side of the cover paper. Do this for all four corners on both covers. Next, cut the corners off, using scissors, at a 45° angle just *outside* this mark. Apply PVA glue to the edges of the cover paper on the left and right and corresponding edges of the cover boards. Leave five to ten minutes for the glue to become tacky.

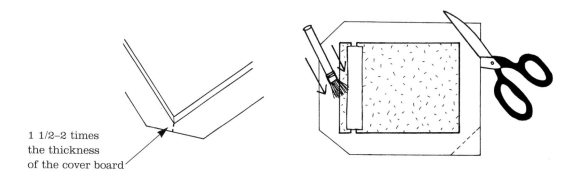

1 1/2–2 times
the thickness
of the cover board

5 Use your fingers and the bone folder to stretch the paper tightly around the edges of the boards to the inside. Cover with nonstick paper and burnish with a bone folder along these two edges and the sides of the cardboard to press out any air bubbles. Wipe off any excess glue.

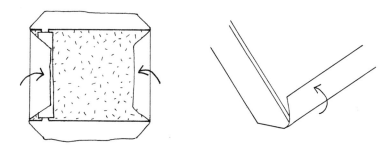

6 Apply glue to the edges of the cover paper and cover boards on the head and tail. While the glue becomes tacky, look closely at how the cover paper is wrapped around the corners. Doing the next step correctly will prevent lumpy corners. Tuck in the cover paper at all four corners (below left); then wrap the newly glued edges around the head and tail. Again, use your fingers and the bone folder to stretch the paper tightly around the edges of the boards. Burnish the paper with the bone folder along these two edges and the sides of the cardboard to avoid a bubble of glue along these edges. Wipe off any excess glue.

Using the book press, or the pressing boards and C-clamps, nip the covers; that is, press tightly and release immediately. If you do not have the tools, skip this step. Discard the used newspaper.

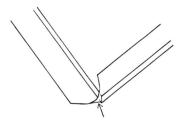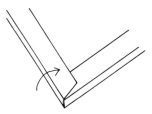

7 Use the spring-loaded dividers or a compass to measure the smallest turn-in on any of the four sides. Set the dividers at this distance. Mark this depth twice on each of the four sides, in pencil (on both covers) measuring from the edge of the cover toward the middle. **Note:** Use of dividers or a compass is the quickest, easiest way to complete this step. By setting the distance once, you can then mark it quickly in sixteen places (eight on each cover). If these tools are not available, use a ruler and measure carefully.

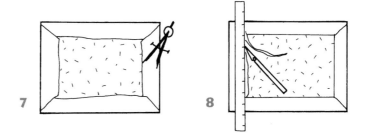

8 Using the craft knife and metal ruler, cut lightly through the irregular edges of the cover paper by aligning the metal ruler with the two marked points on each side. *Do not cut deeply, or you will cut through the board.* Holding the craft knife horizontally, slide the blade under the irregular excess edges of cover paper. Peel off the cut paper edges, and discard them. Because the glue holding these edges has not had time to dry completely, they should pull away from the cardboard with little damage.

If the cover paper is thick, there will be a ridge where it ends on the inside of the cover. If you wish, sand this raised edge with a scrap of fine-grit sandpaper wrapped around your fingertip. Wrap the covers in nonstick paper and then in absorbent scrap paper, and place in a press while preparing the endpapers. The scrap paper absorbs the moisture from the glue through the nonstick paper, and helps prevent the cover from warping as the glue dries.

 ENDPAPERS

Endpapers must be opaque so that the edges of the cover paper will not show through them. Endpapers form a visual transition from the outside of the book (the cover) to the inside.

> **MATERIALS**
> * paper (colored, decorated, or handmade)
> * newspaper
> * paste
> * bristle brush
> * pencil
> * triangle
> * metal ruler
> * craft knife with a new blade
> * cutting mat
> * nonstick paper
> * bone folder

DIRECTIONS

1 Using the triangle, metal ruler, craft knife, and cutting mat, mark with a pencil and then cut two pieces of your chosen paper the same size as the text pages: 11 x 14" (27.5 x 35 cm). (See pages 13–15.)

2 Lay out clean newspaper; then place the endpapers wrong side up on top. Take the covers out of the press and place them nearby. Paste the wrong side of the endpapers, and then center them on the inside of the covers. Adjust the position, if necessary; paste allows you to make adjustments for a short while, which is its main advantage over PVA glue.

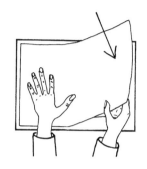

3 Cover the endpapers with nonstick paper, and burnish with the bone folder. Wipe off the excess paste. Wrap the covers in clean nonstick paper, and then in absorbent paper. Press until dry, at least a few hours.

7–3 After restoring this photo album from the late 1800s, the artist replaced the original photographic portraits with eighteen watercolor portraits of cows. The binding is one of the many variations of album binding. Susan Rotolo (United States), *Cows,* 1990. Arches paper, watercolor, leather binding, 5 1/4 x 4 1/4 x 2" (13.3 x 10.8 x 5 cm).

PUNCHING HOLES AND BINDING

MATERIALS
- 2 pieces of scrap paper
- scissors
- pencil
- triangle
- metal ruler
- craft knife with a new blade
- cutting mat
- leather hole punch, 1/16 to 1/8" (1 to 3 mm) and a small hammer (or electric drill, see page 17)
- scrap softwood or thick cardboard, book size or larger
- binding thread (linen is ideal), crochet thread, or the full thickness of embroidery thread
- darning or tapestry needle

DIRECTIONS

1 Using the triangle, metal ruler, craft knife, and cutting mat, mark with a pencil and then cut the two pieces of scrap paper to the same size as the text pages (not including the guards). (See pages 13–15.) Use one of these papers underneath the pages to protect them from damage. On the other scrap paper, measure and mark the placement of the holes for the text pages. Then use this as a template for punching holes in the text (inside) pages and in the covers, as for *Japanese stab-bound books.* (See page 68.)

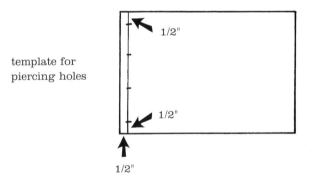

template for piercing holes

1/2"

1/2"

1/2"

2 Cut a length of thread three times the height of the spine, and thread the needle. Enter the lowest hole from the front, and come out the back. Move the needle all the way up to the top hole and enter it from the back and come out the front.

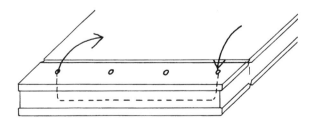

7–4 Sixteen dawn-
to-dusk photographs
of a rock formation
on the Oregon side
of the Columbia
River are mounted in
this album on papers
from India. Anna
Guillemot (United
States), *Fragment of
Eternity,* 1993. Hard
cover, acid-free paper,
leather thong and
beads closure, 6 1/4 x
8 1/2 x 2" (15.6 x 21.2
x 5 cm) when closed.

3   Enter the second hole down from the head from the front through to the
back. Loop around the thread already in place along the back cover, and go back
through the same hole to the front cover.

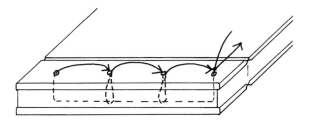

4   Do the same on the third hole down from the head: enter from the front, loop
around the thread already in place along the back cover, and go back through
the same hole to the front cover.

5   Now you are back where you started. Pull the thread tight; then tie the two
threads in a square knot over the lowest hole on the front cover and cut them 1/4"
(6 mm) from the knot. This simple binding allows you to unbind and rebind by
cutting the thread and adding or subtracting pages quickly.

8–1 In this original children's storybook photo album different colors on the pages and spine allow us to clearly see the book's structure. Judy Jacobs (United States), *Raymond Rooster III,* 1994. Concertina-spine binding with inserted pages and fabric-covered boards, 7 x 10 x 2 1/4" (17.8 x 25.4 x 5.7 cm), when closed. Photo: Bill Wickett.

8–2 This original presentation of a concertina book is achieved by placing the tails of the covers together and fanning out the heads. Daphne Dobbyn, bookbinder, and Catriona Montgomery, calligrapher, (Australia), *Lady Windermere's Fan,* 1992. Calligraphy in gouache with transfer gold on paper, 8 3/8 x 3 1/8 x 3/8" (21.2 x 8 x 1 cm), when closed.

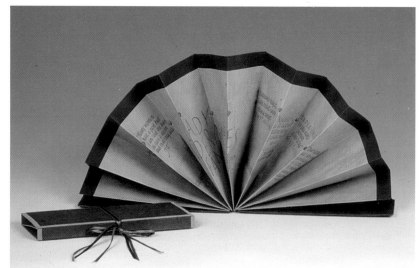

ADVANCED BINDINGS

CONCERTINA BINDING

There is no sewing in concertina (also known as accordion or leporello) books and cards. The binding and pages are formed by the continual length of paper and zigzag folds.

Simple concertinas can make wonderful cards and visual books, because the images can be continuous. A long panoramic drawing can be folded to close into book form. When the book is opened, the sense of the pages having a front or back side vanishes. Concertinas, because of their expandable binding, are suitable for scrapbooks.

front cover   text pages   back cover

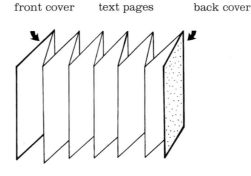

8–3 This seven-page concertina book is stored in a handmade wooden box. Each page represents a member of the artist's family, with images representing each individual's role in the family unit. Rita MacDonald (United States), *Family* (edition of 100), 1994. Pages are screen-printed, 7 3/4 x 16 x 3/8" (19.7 x 40.6 x 1 cm), when closed.

Concertina binding has sculptural possibilities: it can be circular, linear, or curved. Concertinas generally have two hard covers, but if the front and back pages are joined to form a circle, a continuous book form is created. Since a continuous book cannot be closed, it becomes a sculptural piece.

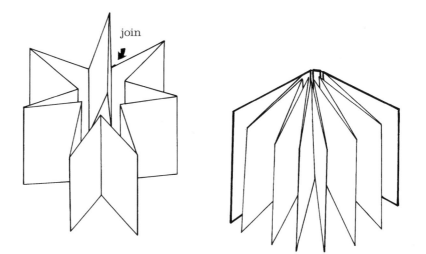

Concertinas can be made from just one strip of paper, which means that beginners can avoid the more complex process of joining strips. These one-strip books will have fewer pages than a concertina with joined strips.

The paper should be opaque and crisp with a strong grain. The stronger grain produces clean, sharp creases. Papers can be 80–100 lb (170–260 gsm) heavy-card weight, or 20–24 lb (80–120 gsm) text weight for small books or cards.

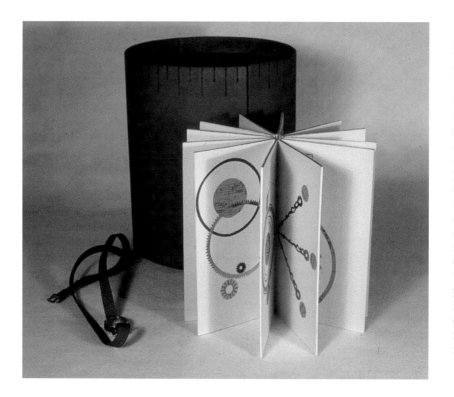

8–4 This 12-page continuous concertina book represents the hours of the day and the cyclical nature of time and music. Gloria Helfgott (United States), *Marking Time*, 1993. A collage of relief prints, drawings, clock parts, sheet music, ink, and acrylic on Arches cover paper and museum board. The cylindrical cover is tooled pigskin (with plastic clock-face numbers) in a cloth-covered box, 7 x 6 1/2 x 6 1/2" (17.8 x 16.5 x 16.5 cm).

MATERIALS

- paper, 22 x 30" (56 x 76 cm), 1 sheet, for text pages
- pencil
- triangle
- metal ruler
- craft knife with a new blade
- cutting mat
- bone folder

DIRECTIONS

1 Sharpen your pencil to a fine point, to make your measurement marks thin and precise. Take your time when measuring. Find the direction of the paper's grain. (The strips will be cut lengthwise across the grain; the folds will be made parallel to the grain, or perpendicular to the length of the strip.) Plan how many strips (two, three, or four) you can cut from the height of the paper. In this example we will use three strips. The height of the strip will be the height of your book. Using a triangle and ruler, mark with a pencil where you plan to cut. (See page 13.)

2 Using a metal ruler, craft knife, and cutting mat, cut the paper into three strips. (See page 15.)

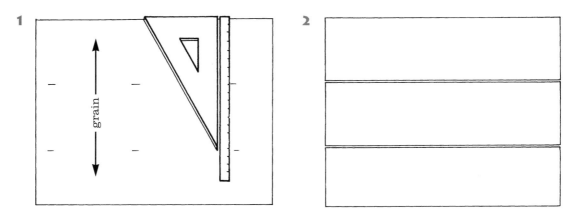

3 Choose one of the long sides of each strip as the head. Lightly mark in pencil an arrow—on both sides of each strip—pointing to this edge. Always line up these edges when folding. When the strips of paper are folded into a book, this edge will be at the head of the book.

Choose how wide you want each page to be, keeping in mind its proportion to the height. Plan for a 1/4" (6 mm) tab on both ends of the strip for gluing to the adjacent page or to the covers. (See page 91 for a guide.) Divide the remaining length of the paper by the page width to see how many pages you will get out of each strip; five pages are ideal.

Find where the fold nearest the center of the strip will be. Use the triangle and the bone folder to score there. Make this fold by lining up the edges marked with arrows; then use the bone folder to smooth the crease. Recheck that the height of the strip of paper is consistent. Sometimes you don't notice that one end is taller than the other until it is folded. If the two ends are different, make them the same by lining up the triangle with one right-angle side straight against the fold; line up the other right-angle side with the shortest edge (from the head to the bottom of the strip). This will reveal the longer edges protruding past the edge of the triangle. Draw a line along the length of the strip of paper. Trim to the line, using the craft knife and metal ruler on the cutting mat.

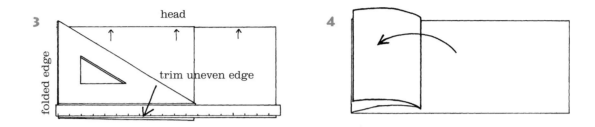

4 Lay the folded strip on the table with the fold on your left, and the open ends to the right. Measure the width of one page from the fold along the head, and mark this point in pencil. Fold the top length of paper to the left at the mark, again lining up the head as you fold. Crease the fold with the bone folder.

If you have a long strip that can accommodate more pages here, fold the top length of paper back to the right directly over the previous fold. Line up to the head. Crease the fold. Continue folding this top length of paper back and forth until there is not enough paper left for another page.

5 Flip the whole concertina over from right to left.

6 Fold the new top length of paper back to the right directly above the previous fold. Line up the length of the paper to the head; fold and crease the paper with the bone folder.

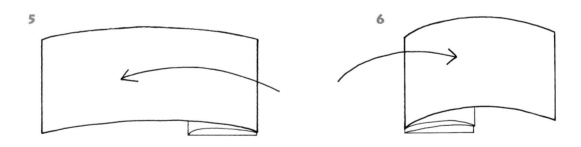

7 Fold the top length of paper to the left. Continue folding this top length of paper back and forth until there is not enough paper left for another page. Each time, make the fold directly above the one below, and line up to the head. Fold the other two strips of paper in the same way. Leave a 1/4" (6 mm) tab on both ends of each strip.

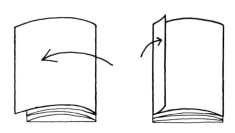

7

8 Look at this diagram for a concertina book. This is just a model. You can have any number of pages in your book. Sometimes you will need to cut off a tab at the end of a strip so that the three sections of the concertina match the diagram. Measure and check carefully before cutting.

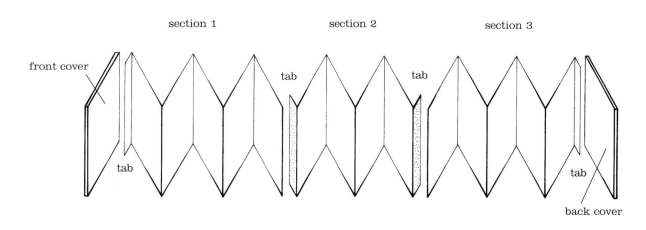

section 1 section 2 section 3

front cover

tab tab

tab

tab

back cover

JOINING CONCERTINA PAGES

MATERIALS
- folded text pages
- newspaper
- paste and brush (or glue stick)
- nonstick paper
- book press or two C-clamps and two pressing boards (optional)

DIRECTIONS

1 You will paste the tabs to connect the strips. For ease of use in a classroom, you may use a glue stick instead of paste. Glue and glue sticks are not as strong as paste, but are less messy to work with. First, slightly *miter* the top and bottom edges of each tab; that is, cut the tab at a slight angle at the top and the bottom as shown at right.

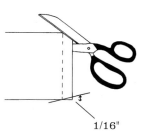

1/16"

2 Lay out clean newspaper on the work surface. Fold a scrap piece of paper in half, and place it so that it covers the page and just a fraction past the fold, exposing only the tab; doing this prevents paste from getting on the pages. Paste the tab thoroughly, working the paste into the paper with the brush. Discard the scrap paper.

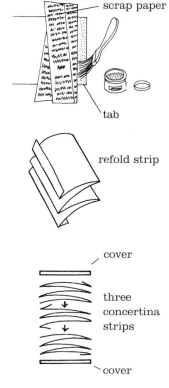

scrap paper

tab

refold strip

cover

three concertina strips

cover

3 Refold the pasted page, and place on a clean surface, pasted tab up. Note which edge of each strip is the head (earlier, you marked this with an arrow), and lay the strips out in sequence, with the heads up.

4 Place a small scrap of nonstick paper under the tab. Place the end of the second strip in position on top of the tab. Refold this strip, still on top. Check that all the folds line up vertically. Make minor adjustments. Press the tab in place to help it adhere. Discard the scraps of nonstick paper and newspaper that have paste on them. Paste the other tab to connect the third strip the same way. As you work, check that the strips line up squarely. Wrap all the text pages in nonstick paper and then in absorbent scrap paper. (This wicks away moisture to prevent warping as the paste dries.) Press the pages, or put them under a weight while working on the covers.

MAKING SEPARATE COVERS

MATERIALS
- cardboard or mat board
- paper for covers and endpapers
- pencil
- triangle
- metal ruler
- craft knife with a new blade
- cutting mat
- newspaper
- bone folder
- PVA glue and stencil brush
- nonstick paper
- book press or 2 C-clamps and 2 pressing boards (optional)
- spring-loaded dividers or compass
- paste and brush

DIRECTIONS
If you are a beginner, you can do a version of this that skips wrapping covers and adding endpapers. Instead of plain cardboard, use mat-board scraps that are colored on one side and white on the other (or use cardboard that is white on one side). Picture framers use mat board and often give away unused scraps. You can buy full sheets from a framer or an art supplier. If using mat board, do only steps 1, 4, and 6.

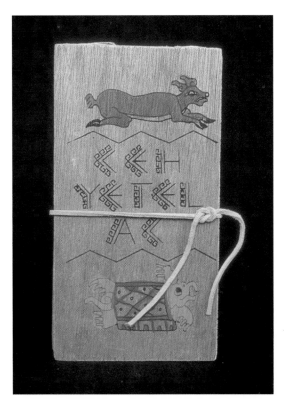

8–6a, b A story by Alejandra Kim Bolles was written in the old Mayan language, serigraphed (silk-screened) and then hand-painted on paper made by Mayan craftspeople of the Yucatan. Mark A. Callaghan (Mexico), 1995. Plant-fiber paper, 8 3/4 x 4 3/4 x 5/8" (22 x 11.9 x 1.5 cm).

8–5 This book was created as a visual expression of the nature of life as a journey unique to each individual. Susan Hensel (United States), *Infinite Loops,* 1993. Laminated handmade text paper, airbrushed and stamped original text, 4 x 28" (10.2 x 71.1 cm).

1   To determine the correct size for the cover boards, measure the height and width of the text pages and add 1/8" (3 mm) to the length and width. Cut the boards for the covers to this size. Check that the grain runs head to tail. The squares, or the amount the covers extend beyond the text pages, are very small in concertina books.

2   Choose the paper for wrapping the covers; it may be plain, or a paper you have decorated yourself. Add 2" (50 mm) to the length and width of the cover boards to determine the size of the cover papers. This will leave 1" (25 mm) on each side to wrap around the boards. Using the triangle, metal ruler, craft knife, and cutting mat, mark with a pencil and then cut the cover paper to size. (See page 13–15.) Center the boards on the paper, and trace their position lightly in pencil.

Lay clean newspaper on the work surface. Glue the boards on one side, and place them on the cover papers. Burnish them flat with a bone folder. Cut the corners of the cover paper at a 45° angle, and glue the edges of the cover paper, wrapping them around the boards: the sides first, and then the top and bottom. (See page 80–81; the process is the same except that concertina covers do not have hinges.) Wipe off any excess glue. Burnish the cover paper on the edges as well as the sides of the cardboard. Wrap the covers individually in nonstick paper. Nip the covers in a press to help the papers adhere (press tightly and release immediately; see page 21). If you do not have a press, skip this step. Afterward, remove the nonstick paper.

3   Place both covers on the work surface. Trim the turned-in edges to make them equal. Use spring-loaded dividers or a compass to measure the shortest point of the turn-ins. Mark this distance lightly in pencil on all four sides of both covers. Use the craft knife and metal ruler to cut along these marks. Slide the blade of the craft knife under the excess uneven edge to lift it up; discard these edges.

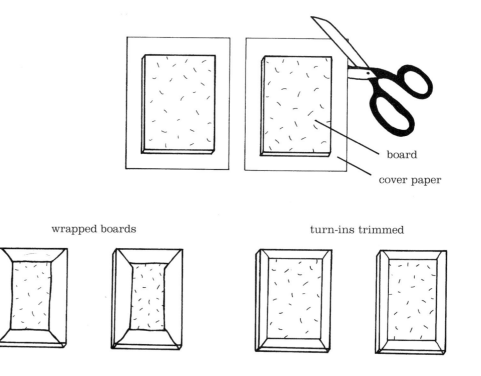

board

cover paper

wrapped boards   turn-ins trimmed

4 Take the text pages out of the press, if you used one. Work on clean newspaper, and connect the pages to the boards by using a folded piece of scrap paper to mask off all but the tab on the first text page (see page 92, step 2 for joining the pages). Paste the tab thoroughly. Discard the used scrap paper and newspaper. Place a small scrap of nonstick paper under the tab. Place the front cover on the table. Place the folded text pages squarely on top, with the pasted tab down. Position carefully and check that the squares on all sides are even. Lay out clean newspaper and repeat these steps to paste the tab on the other end of the text pages to the back cover. Press to adhere, and check that both covers line up exactly. Make any adjustments you feel are necessary.

5 Cut two endpapers to the same height and width as one page. The grain of the paper should run head to tail. Working on clean newspaper, apply paste to the wrong side of the endpapers, and then flip them over and position them on the inside of the covers. The endpapers will hide where the tabs are attached to the covers. Wrap the covers inside and out in nonstick paper and absorbent scrap paper, and put in a press or under a weight. Press overnight.

6 Discard the absorbent scrap paper and nonstick paper, and erase all the pencil marks inside the book. Your concertina book is done!

CONCERTINA BINDING WITH CONNECTED COVERS

Concertinas can be bound into two connected covers instead of two separate covers. This binding makes the concertina look and function more like a codex (Western-style book). A wide hinge, formed by cover paper that connects the covers, allows for the full thickness of the text pages of the book, the thickness of both cover boards, and anything that will be glued into the book after it is made. This wide hinge also becomes the spine. Once bound in the connected covers, the book is no longer expandable. However, it is a little more durable than a simple concertina, since there is more support for the pages.

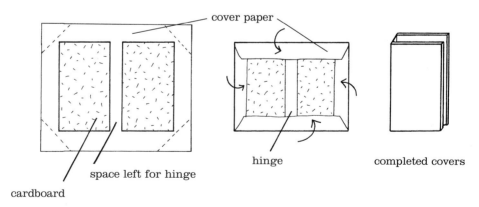

cover paper

cardboard

space left for hinge

hinge

completed covers

The text pages and the boards for the cover are made the same way as those for the simple concertina. The width of the cover paper will be the width of the two cover boards plus the space for the spine (described above) plus 2" (50 mm). The height is that of the cover boards plus 2" (50 mm). This allows 1" (25 mm) all around for wrapping around the covers. Glue the boards on the cover paper, leaving the full width for the hinge. Wrap the boards as before; however, both covers are now connected.

To attach the text pages, paste one end tab, and place the pages in position between the covers (with the tabs near the spine). Paste the second end tab, and close the cover onto it. Try opening the book and turning pages, making adjustments as needed. Add endpapers, wrap, and press overnight.

8–7 Three layers of concertina pages with connected covers are displayed in a format called a star or carousel book. The outside pages are cut out to reveal the images behind them. One of a series of works using children's book structures to make books for adults. Larry Thomas (United States), *Stories Without End,* 1994. Photocopy and collage on commercial papers, 7 1/4 x 3 1/4 x 1 1/2" (18.4 x 8.3 x 3.7 cm), when closed.

CONCERTINA SPINE BINDING WITH INSERTED PAGES

For this book, a narrow concertina is used for the binding only, and each page is a separate piece of paper pasted into the concertina. (See fig. 8–1 for an example.) This makes the book ideal for displaying handmade paper samples, photos, a postcard collection, or any flat pages that you want to see on both sides. The binding is expandable to allow for the thickness of whatever you add to it, and the cover can be hard or soft.

MATERIALS
- 70–80 lb (160–180 gsm) paper, 1 large sheet, for the concertina
- paper for covers and endpapers
- cardboard or mat board
- nonstick paper
- newspaper
- book press or 2 C-clamps and 2 pressing boards (optional)
- PVA glue and stencil brush
- paste and brush

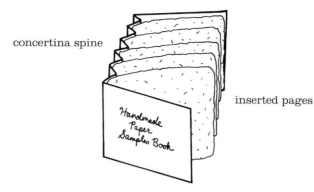

concertina spine

inserted pages

DIRECTIONS

1 First, determine the size of the book. Collect all the items to be mounted in the book in a neat pile. They can be different heights and widths or all the same size. Measure the height of the tallest piece and the width of the widest piece. The book should be about 1/4" (5–7 mm) higher and 1/2" (12 mm) wider than the largest of the items it will hold. Make a note of the dimensions.

2 Count the number of pieces your book will include. This determines how many pages, and consequently, how many mountain and valley folds are needed. The larger the paper, the fewer joins will be necessary.

3 Since the concertina is just for the binding, not for the pages, it will be narrow. A 5/8–7/8" (15–20 mm) concertina is wide enough. To create the concertina (see page 89), score, fold, and crease the strip of paper. Doing this accurately does take practice, so be patient with yourself.

4 Decide whether you want a hard or a soft cover. A soft cover can be a continuing part of the long strip of paper used to make the concertina, or it can be cut separately from any heavy paper. Soft or hard covers are then pasted or glued to the tabs on each end of the narrow concertina spine. Paste dries more slowly than glue and gives you more time to work, but either can be used.

Make a hard cover as you would make separate covers. (See page 92). Paste the endpapers in, hiding the tabs. Wrap the book in nonstick paper and absorbent scrap paper, and nip in a press or place under a weight until dry. When the glue and paste are dry, take the book out and unwrap it. The book itself is now complete, except for gluing in the items.

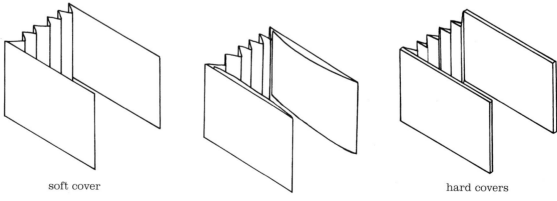

soft cover

soft cover with turn-ins

hard covers

5 Decide on the order of the pieces for the book. Lay out clean newspaper on the work surface. Take the first "page" to be glued in and turn it facedown. Mask off, with scrap paper, all but 1/2" (12 mm) along the edge that will attach to the spine. Apply glue (or paste) to this edge, and then place the page in position in the concertina binding. Put nonstick paper in the fold behind this page. Glue (or paste) all the other pages the same way, placing them in the binding with nonstick paper between each fold. Wrap the whole book in nonstick paper and absorbent scrap paper. Press overnight.

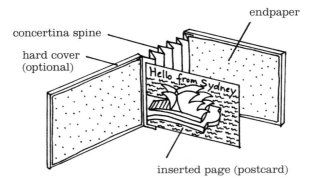

inserted page (postcard)

 TUNNEL BOOKS

Tunnel books are made by connecting pages between two opposing concertinas, which are made the same as concertinas with inserted pages. One edge of each page is glued to the first concertina; then the opposite edge of the page is glued to the second concertina. The illustration shows a partially completed tunnel book; the right-hand side of the pages have not yet been glued to the concertina binding on the right.

Though the process of assembling tunnel books is not so different from that for the concertina spine binding with inserted pages, the design process takes planning and practice. Tunnel books are little dioramas, or stage sets, with each layer of scenery forming a page between the concertinas. The viewer looks through the areas cut open on the front page to see the images or shapes behind. The opening in the first page must be large enough to allow this. The first page frames the work and can depict a doorway, window, gate, or pair of curtains. The areas covered by the front page, and each successive page, will cover that portion of all the pages that follow.

CREATIVE IDEAS

• This kind of book lends itself to translucent and transparent materials. Photocopy or draw different parts of a scene onto individual sheets of acetate, and then bind them to create a complete three-dimensional scene. Use layers of tracing paper as clouds or as a succession of snow-covered hills.

• Cut apart one image, and mount the sections on successive pages. Create depth by placing the background on the last page.

8–8 A tunnel book. Dottie Aukofer (United States), *Tree,* 1993. Intaglio print on handmade paper, 12 x 8 x 1" (30.5 x 20.3 x 2.5 cm).

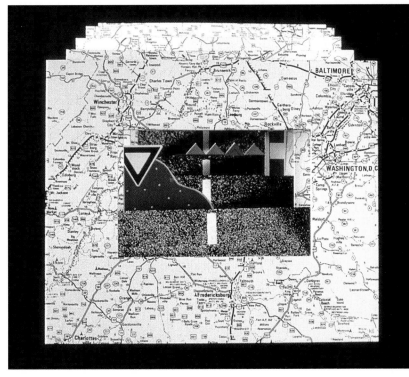

8–9 This tunnel book's inner binding strip becomes a road image—charting a trip across the United States—when the book is fully extended. Carol Barton (United States), *Everyday Road Signs* (edition of 80), 1988. Silkscreened images with offset map pages on commercial paper, 7 1/4 x 8 5/8 x 10" (18.4 x 21.9 x 25.4 cm).

CONCERTINA SPINE BINDING WITH PAMPHLETS SEWN IN

This binding is called a *complex binding* because it uses a combination of two binding techniques—concertina and pamphlet. It can be used for a group of newsletters, theater programs, letters, or cards. The book will open out flat. When you look at the inside of the book, the folds that point up are the mountain folds. Sew into the mountains of the concertina if you are planning to glue other items into the book later; otherwise, sew into either the mountains or the valleys. Sewing into the mountains is often preferable because nothing will be hidden by the folds of the concertina.

MATERIALS
- metal ruler
- newspaper
- scissors
- pencil
- cutting mat
- awl, sharp needle, or compass point
- sewing thread
- darning or tapestry needle

DIRECTIONS

1   Measure the height of the highest card or other item to be bound. Add 1/4" (5 mm–7 mm) to determine the height of the cover and spine, which is usually no more than 12" (30.5 cm). Measure the widest item, and add 1/2" (12 mm) to the width (for squares). If you are sewing into the mountain folds, also add the width of the concertina spine. (See illustration on page 101).

Count the number of items; then make the correct number of valley and mountain folds in the concertina to allow for them. If you have more than twenty items, divide them into two or more books.

2   Make the concertina spine and covers the same way as for inserted pages. (See page 96.) Paste the tabs on the concertina and connect them to the covers. Make hard covers if you wish.

8–10 This complex binding is made of pamphlets sewn into a concertina book. Scenes from an opera are pictured, and a compact disc of the performance is enclosed. Claire Van Vliet (United States), *Dido & Aeneas*, 1989. Handmade paper, 14 5/8 x 70 3/4 x 1" (37.1 x 179.7 x 2.5 cm), when closed. Made at McGregor & Vinzani, Maine.

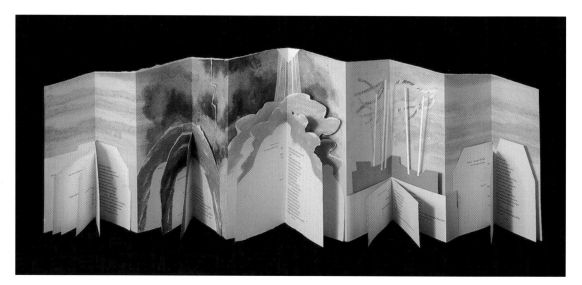

8–11a, b This collection of favorite Christmas cards is sewn into a concertina spine binding. This keeps the cards neatly together and protects them from damage. The tab across the back of the binding gives the book extra support. Jean G. Kropper (Australia), 1994. Heavyweight Canson papers, 9 3/8 x 7 x 1" (24 x 17.7 x 2.5 cm), when closed. Photo: E. Lancaster.

3 Look at the height of the book, and consider the weight and height of the items to be sewn in later. You will sew each item individually to a mountain or valley fold, using the pamphlet binding method. (See page 64.) Decide if you need three or five holes for the pamphlet binding. The taller and heavier the items, the more holes—and stitches—will be needed in the binding to support them.

4 Make a template for the sewing stations. Cut a piece of scrap paper to the same height as the book, and fold it in half. The width of the template is not important. Measure halfway between the top and the bottom of the height. Mark this clearly on the crease in the template. Measure up and down equally for three or five holes, depending on what you have chosen, and mark these points (as for pamphlet binding) on the crease.

5 Stretch the concertina out flat on the cutting mat. Hold the template against each mountain or valley fold, and pierce it in line with each mark. Be consistent. Work through all the folds. Then use the template to pierce holes in each of the items, taking care to keep them in order.

6 Now you are ready to sew. Start at the first fold, and choose the first item. Cut a thread twice as long as the book's height, and thread the needle.

7 Bind the items by sewing each one with the pamphlet binding (see page 66), through both the item and the successive mountains or valleys of the concertina.

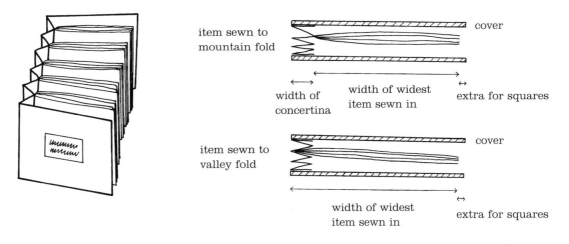

determining the width of the covers

item sewn to mountain fold

cover

width of concertina

width of widest item sewn in

extra for squares

item sewn to valley fold

cover

width of widest item sewn in

extra for squares

SUPPORTING THE BINDING

Concertina spine bindings—with inserted pages or pamphlets—sometimes need more support. This can happen if the concertina is long or the items glued in are heavy. To provide more support, add a strip of cover paper across the binding to limit how much the binding opens out. You may use one or more strips.

MATERIALS

- completed concertina-bound book with inserted pages or pamphlets sewn in
- cover paper, or 1" (25 mm) wide, woven-fabric tape or ribbon
- metal ruler
- PVA glue and stencil brush
- nonstick paper
- newspaper
- bone folder
- craft knife with a new blade
- cutting mat
- pencil
- nonstick paper
- book press or 2 C-clamps and 2 pressing boards (optional)

DIRECTIONS

1 Measure a strip of cover paper 2" (50 mm) wide. The length is determined by the spine of the book. Press the book closed and measure the width of the spine, including the thickness of the covers; then add 2" (50 mm). This allows for an inch-wide connecting tab on each side. Cut the strip. If you are using fabric tape or ribbon, cut it to the determined length. Fold the strip in half lengthwise to make it 1" (25 mm) wide, and working on newspaper, glue it together with PVA glue. Use nonstick paper and burnish with the bone folder.

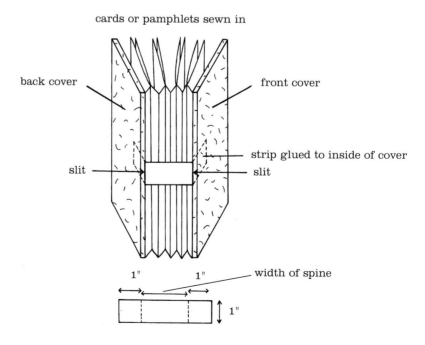

2 In the crease between the front cover and the concertina binding, measure and mark the point halfway between the head and the tail of the book. From this point, measure up—and then down—1/2" (12 mm), and mark each point in pencil. Cut a slit between the two marks; the strip of cover paper or tape will go through here. Do the same for the back cover.

3 Score and fold the tabs 1" (25 mm) at each end, and push them through the slits from the outside of the spine. Then brush PVA glue on one of the tabs, on the side facing the inside of the cover, and press into place. Cover with nonstick paper and burnish with the bone folder. Wipe off excess glue; then put a new piece of nonstick paper over the tab. Repeat this step on the other cover. Place in the press or under a weight for an hour.

COPTIC BINDING

A Coptic binding opens out flat, has several sections, and looks like a Western-style book (codex), except that it has an exposed spine. The covers are the same size as the text pages—there are no squares (overhang). The sewing is more complicated than that for other bindings, and pages cannot be added later; text and covers are bound together. Coptic bindings can be used for address books, diaries, class notes, or a collection of magazines or newsletters. This binding technique suits sculptural books and creative uses of differently shaped pages and colored papers. Pockets and glued-in photos are not appropriate for these books, because their added thickness is difficult to accommodate in the binding.

For lined paper, use commercially made notebooks. Take out any staples, divide the pages into equal sections of ten to twenty folios, and bind them by sewing with a curved needle.

8–12 Coptic books have exposed bindings and are easy to write in because they open out flat. Pages of different colors or shapes can be used to make Coptic books unique. Jean G. Kropper, calligraphy by Olive Bull (Australia), 1995. Various colored and decorated papers; smallest book: 2 3/8 x 4 1/3 x 1" (6 x 10.8 x 2.5 cm); largest book: 8 1/4 x 6 x 3/4" (21 x 15 x 2 cm).

MATERIALS

- text pages
- pencil
- triangle
- metal ruler
- craft knife with a new blade
- cutting mat
- cardboard or mat board
- paper for covers and endpapers
- paste and brush
- nonstick paper
- newspaper
- awl

DIRECTIONS

1 Find the grain direction of the paper you have chosen for the text pages: the folds will be parallel to the grain and to the spine. Using the triangle, metal ruler, craft knife, and cutting mat, mark with a pencil and then cut and fold the papers into an even number of sections (six to twelve). (See pages 13–15.) If you have too few sections, you cannot see the pattern of the sewing.

2 Cut the boards for hard covers to the same dimensions as the text-page sections. Cover the boards as you would for a concertina book (see page 92). Paste the endpapers on the inside of the covers. Wrap the covers in nonstick paper and then absorbent paper, and press. You can make unusual hard covers from materials such as wood, sheets of metal, or Plexiglas™. For a soft cover, use a folio of cover paper with height and width equal to that of the sections.

3 For a template, cut one extra folio from scrap paper. Decide how many rows of stitching you need, and how they will be spaced. The first sewing stations should be about 1/2" (12 mm) from the head and the tail. The next station should be no more than 1/2–3/4" (12–15 mm). The rest of the sewing stations can be placed as you wish, but they should not be more than 1 1/4" (30 mm) apart. Often there are three sewing stations spaced across the middle of the book, but you can have as many as you like. If the book is tall or has heavy covers or many sections, plan extra sewing stations. If it is short, with lightweight covers and few sections, plan fewer sewing stations. Measure and mark the sewing stations on the valley (inside) crease of the template. Mark "head" on top of template (and keep it oriented the same way).

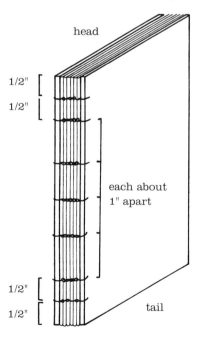

head

1/2"

1/2"

each about 1" apart

1/2"

1/2"

tail

4 Now pierce the holes in all the sections to match the holes in the template. Slip the template inside the first section, and square it up with the pages. Lay the section on the cutting mat. Open the section and hold one side of it up at a 90° angle. Hold the awl at a 45° angle to the pages, and pierce each hole through the mark on the template and all the pages in the section. (See page 65.)

5 The holes in the hard cover should be about 3/16" (3–5 mm) in from the spine edge, and must be exactly even with the corresponding holes marked on the template. Lay the folded template on the front of the front cover, with its left edge 3/16" (3–5 mm) in from the cover's left edge. Mark the holes in pencil on the cover, even with the holes in the template. Put the template aside. Put the front and back covers on top of each other, right sides together. Pierce the holes as marked, through both covers.

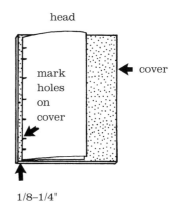

head

mark holes on cover

cover

1/8–1/4"

6 Lay the sections in order, and work sequentially.

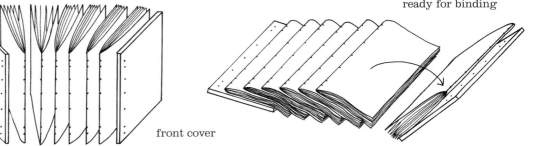

sections

back cover

front cover

front cover and first section, ready for binding

⭐ BINDING THE SECTIONS TOGETHER

MATERIALS
- completed covers and sections, holes punched and pages in order
- curved sewing needle or bookbinding needle
- thread, linen or cotton
- beeswax
- scissors
- nonstick paper
- newspaper
- book press or 2 C-clamps and 2 pressing boards (optional)

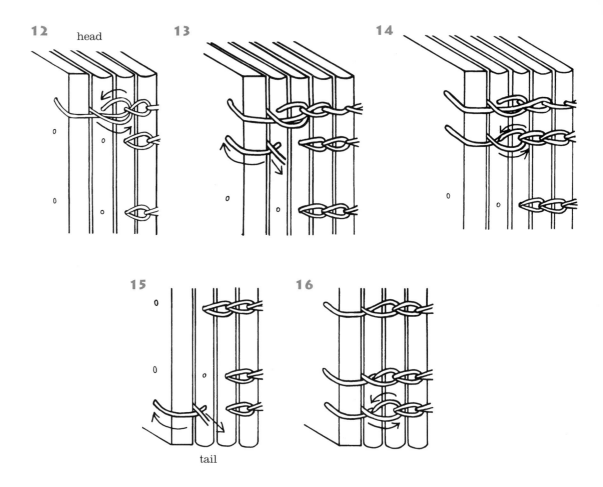

12 Sew around the stitch between the previous two sections from underneath toward the head, and then into the top hole of the last section. You are now inside the top of the last section.

13 Go through the second hole from the inside to the outside of the section. Tighten the previous stitch before going on, remembering to pull the thread parallel to the spine. Enter the second hole on the back cover from the outside. You will come out the inside of the back cover over the stitch you have just made.

14 Sew around the stitch between the two previous sections from underneath toward the head, and then back into the second hole on the last section. Continue down to the next hole, and the hole after that, repeating the same stitch to the lowest sewing station, at the tail. Tighten the previous stitch each time before going on.

15 Repeat the same stitch at the lowest hole by the tail.

16 Go back into the same hole, as before, and tie a square knot. Cut the ends of the thread about 1/4" (5–7 mm) from the knot.

17 Wrap in nonstick paper and then absorbent paper, and put in a press or under a weight. Press overnight. The next day, take your book out of the press, unwrap it, and celebrate completing your first *Coptic book*. Look it over with an objective eye. Flip the pages and look at the binding. Is the sewing evenly tight? How is the tension? If it is too loose, the book will flop; if it is too tight, the book will splay open. Are there any things you would design differently if you made this book again?

CREATIVE IDEA
Add beads to the stitching on the outside of the sections.

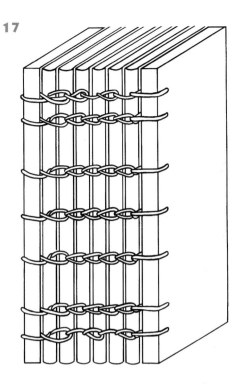

17

OOPS! MY THREAD IS TOO SHORT!
First, relax. Coptic bindings use a long thread, so it is common to run short. A weaver's knot is designed to join a new sewing thread to one that is too short. The knot is tied inside the book so that it is not seen. (If you have to go back a stitch so that the thread is on the inside of a section, do so.) All you need is 1–1 1/4" (25–30 mm) of thread left, although the knot is easier to tie with a longer thread.

1 Form a loose half hitch near one end of the new length of thread.

2 Loop the long end of this new thread back through the half hitch. Do not tighten it yet.

3 Drop this loop over the old thread. Gradually slide the half hitch close to the old thread, closing the loop around it and making sure the loop is as close to the base of the old thread as possible. (This ensures that the knot will not interfere with the next stitch.) Tighten completely. Cut off any extra threads 3/8" (10 mm) from the knot. Thread the long end of the new thread on the needle. Continue binding.

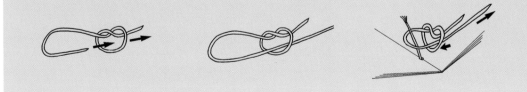

9

9–1 A small Japanese stab-bound book hangs from each of the four sides of this pyramid. The horizontal cardboard shapes can be lifted off the top to allow the sides to open out flat. Michael Jacobs (United States), *Two Triangle Ritual Books,* 1995. Sides made from mat board covered with bamboo paper, bone beads, 8 1/2 x 5 1/2 x 5 1/2" (21.6 x 14 x 14 cm). Photo: Bill Wickett

9–2 Layers of text from newspapers, the Bible, and other sources are embedded in silk to reveal messages both universal and personal. Sand, ground marble, and ash are added to convey the sense that the book is from the depths of time or deep within the artist. Marie-Claire Meier (Switzerland), *Message II,* 1993. Handmade paper, silk, metal, 11 7/8 x 13 x 2 3/4" (30 x 33 x 7 cm).

CREATIVE DEPARTURES

ALTERNATIVE FORMATS

A book's *format* is its design, which includes its size, style, page layout, typography, and binding. For your handmade books, choose a format that best suits and supports your message.

Book artist Edward Hutchins explains: "Instead of trying to fit the text, illustrations, design, and structure into a conventional format, I try to answer the question: What is the best way to get the message across? ...[L]ook for the connection between the structure, the message, and the visual presentation. If I have done my job, they can't be separated."

SCROLLS

Scrolls, usually made of paper, can be horizontal or vertical. They can be tiny and fit wrapped around an empty spool or a length of dowel, or they can be large sculptural pieces. Scrolls can roll up and be tied with a cord—or fit in a bottle, metal cigar tube, film canister, or an empty flashlight. Scrolls can be made for a proclamation, a tall tale, a calligraphy painting, or a treasure map.

CREATIVE IDEA

Write a secret message from the point of view of a spy working undercover in a war zone. Choose the war, the country, the date of the message, and the nationality, age, and gender of the spy. To whom is the spy writing and what is the important message?

9–3 The format of these 50-inch-long paper scrolls suits the telling of a long tale that gradually unfolds as you read it. Emily McVarish (United States), *Stance,* 1993. Letterpress printed, ends glued to and wound around wooden spindles, tied with a silk ribbon, 4 1/2 x 2 3/4" (11.4 x 7 cm).

9–4 This fan was made from cards from the Gaultier Paris boutique. The cards bear no identification; the fashion house assumes that the viewer will recognize the designer's work. Suellen Glashausser (United States), *Gaultier Fan with Box,* 1991. Fan made from tin-edged Gaultier cards, stored in a box made of cardboard and tin, 12 x 2 x 1" (30 x 5 x 2.5 cm), when closed.

 FANS

The fan, like the scroll, is an early book form. Several strips the same length are loosely bound through a hole at one end with a tie, ring, nut and bolt, loop of wire, or rivet. A fan lets the reader view almost any mix of pages at once, allowing for comparison of the information on the sections. Current uses of this format are color swatches of paint or fabric, or for cooling yourself on a hot day. Because the viewer can open the fan to any section or sections at one time, the binder cannot control the sequencing.

CREATIVE IDEAS

• Glue one image on cardboard, and cut it into strips. Punch a hole near the end of each strip (in the same position on each) and bind them together as a fan. See the effect of viewing the image this way. Vary the fan form by punching one hole in the center of each strip for a double fan; or one hole staggered along the strips to form an irregular fan shape.

• Find an old magazine with lots of photos. Cut out several small images of the same thing (flowers, eyes, or car tires, for example). Glue the sequence of these same images on the panels of the fan with a glue stick or PVA glue. A rhythm of the repetition of the images is formed.

• Experiment with different shapes for the sections of a fan.

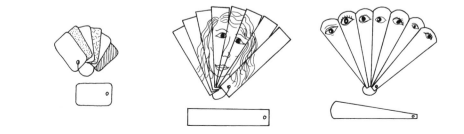

BLINDS

This format has been used in many tropical regions. Palm fronds are cut into strips and incised with writing and images to tell stories. Cords pass through the hole or holes in each strip and hold the blind together. The ends of the cords have a coin, bead, or charm attached, which stops the cords from pulling through. (See fig. 1–3a, b on page 2.)

CREATIVE IDEAS

• Glue a photo or image onto cardboard, and cut it into strips of equal width and length for a blind. Punch two or three holes in the same position on each blind, and connect the blinds with a cord. Place one hole in the center and one hole close to both ends, or vary their position for different effects.

• Experiment with cutting the image into strips, sliding the strips out of alignment with one another, and then mounting them onto cardboard. Or, mount drawing papers onto cardboard and make into a blind; then draw your own visual story onto the strips.

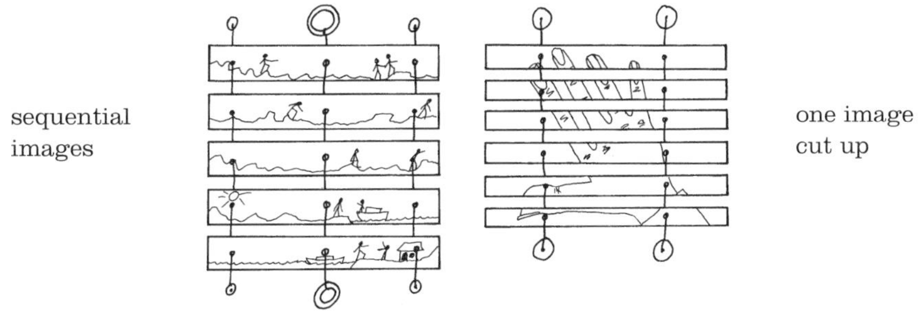

sequential images

one image cut up

9–5 An artist's book exploring outer space imagery and the color blue: oval pages of black Arches paper are bound with chiffon string in the blind format. There is sequential visual content but no written text. Deborah Phillips Chodoff (United States), *Blue Black Book,* 1990. Gouache, acrylic and metallic paints, rubbings, stamping, and found objects, 29 1/2 x 14 1/2 x 1 1/2" (74.9 x 36.8 x 3.8 cm).

9–6 Stories of courtship, relationships, and sex are told through the metaphor of entering a house. The dos-à-dos format (with Coptic binding) suits the telling of two sides of one story. Joan M. Soppe (United States), *About the Linens* (edition of 10), 1995. Copper wire; pages made from glassine envelopes, handmade and other papers, intaglio printing, letterpress, hand sewing, collage, and found objects, 5 1/2 x 4 x 2" (14 x 10.2 x 5 cm), when closed.

 ## DOS-À-DOS, OR BACK-TO-BACK

This is an old, traditional format for binding together two well-paired books or two volumes. The reader looks at one side and then flips over the whole book to look at the other side. The two sides share a back cover.

Use pamphlet, Japanese stab, album, or Coptic binding for a *dos-à-dos*. For the pamphlet binding, bend one length of cover paper into a zigzag, and sew the sections into the two valley folds. For Japanese stab, album, or Coptic binding, the two books have the middle cover board in common. Bind the first book as usual; then lay it on a table, front cover down, with the spine on the right. Use the book's back cover as the back cover of the second book, which you will bind down the left side. Put endpapers on both sides of the middle cover. When either one of the books is right side up, the other is upside-down. (See fig. 10–27 on page 140.)

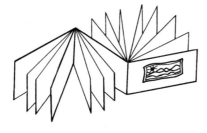 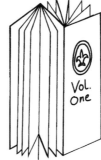 

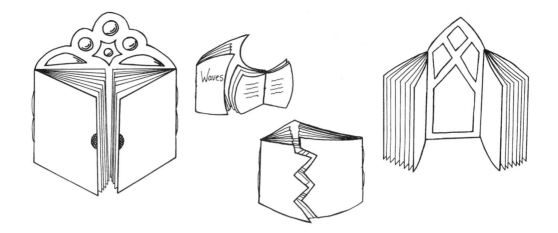

 ## FRENCH DOORS

This format evokes early Christian icons, with a central panel and two sides that fold out, like a double gate or French doors. For books, this format is suitable for "parallel" stories, two stories that take place at the same time. Or, the format can recount two sides of one story; for example, a "his and her" version of an event. The reader can shift between the books, or read one and then the other; the binder has little control over the sequence in which the reader views the mix of pages.

9–7 This birthday card uses a French-door format, shown closed and tied with a ribbon (left) and open (right). Jean G. Kropper with calligraphy by Olive Bull (Australia), 1995. Hand-printed linocut on Arches paper, 11 x 6" (28.7 x 15 cm).

9–8 Each scroll, decorated with watermark drawings, embedded eggshell, tea, and mica, rolls up into its own separate box. Robbin Ami Silverberg (United States), *Scrolls,* 1994. Installation view as exhibited at the Museum of Applied Arts in Budapest, Hungary. Pulp-sprayed flax paper, 30 x 2' (9.1 x .6 m).

 ## LARGE BOOKS

Books that exceed standard sizes create their own environment and become sculpture; people compare the size of the book to their own size. Large books are rarely for private or personal messages; they are usually made for more public statements.

If you plan to make a large book, consider how you will transport it. Structural concerns are crucial for a large book to function properly. You do not want your book to fall apart when readers turn the pages. Making a large book could be a group project, with each person designing a page and helping with the binding.

MINIATURE BOOKS

Miniature books, less than 3" (75 mm) high or wide, have a charm all their own and are often a favorite of collectors. They are cute and portable, and they can be hidden in a pocket, but attention to detail in their construction is critical. These books can be made of expensive materials because so little is needed. The books are suitable for fables, children's stories, personal stories, on-the-spot accounts of an event, and pocket guidebooks.

9–9 This miniature fine-press book reflects the artist's fascination with stories of the Revolutionary War's early battles. Eric Hanson (Australia), *General Gage's Instructions*, 1974. Letterpress-printed, 2 3/4 x 2 1/8 x 1/2" (7 x 5.5 x 1 cm), when closed.

ARTISTS' BOOKS

An *artist's book* is a book made by an artist, but it can also be a book that is a piece of art in itself, or a book that takes artistic issues into consideration. Artists' books might use writing or images, or neither, or both to tell a story; or they might simply be sculptural pieces. The artist often combines many techniques in imaginative ways to communicate a message.

9–10 This one-of-a-kind artist's book was designed to enshrine natural materials gathered on a trip through the Sierra Nevada mountains. Karen Stahlecker (United States), *Golden Shrine*, 1995. Shaped book with perforated covers, artist's handmade papers, natural materials, 7 1/4 x 4 1/4 x 1 1/3" (18.4 x 10.8 x 3.5 cm), when closed.

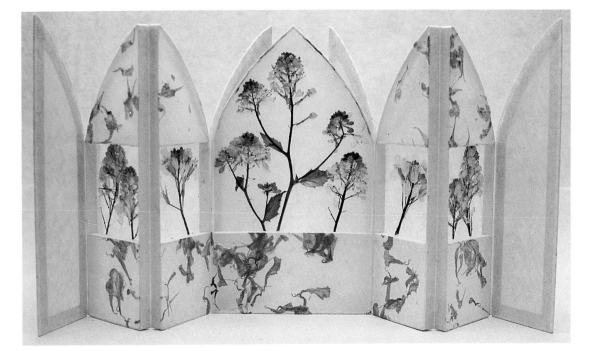

DIFFERENT PERSPECTIVES

People see books from different points of view. An author sees a book for its literary *content*, or what is written in it. A traditional craft bookbinder sees a book as a carefully constructed *object* and judges how well it is made. An artist sees a book as a *concept* or *symbol* and judges its form or overall message.

Books generally cover a combination of these three perspectives. Artists' books, including sculptural books and altered books, draw from these perspectives but emphasize art and concept; many commercially printed books consider art only as a vehicle for the literary content. Commercially made books are bound in hardcover or softcover, and in one format—the codex.

What forms will *your* books take? Where will they be displayed? In a library? Bookstore? Museum? Art gallery? Craft shop? Will they be picked up and read or handled; or be studied and admired? Will they be considered literature, craft, art, or a combination?

New means of communication have challenged the traditional book form. Information previously conveyed in books can now be presented as a CD-ROM or video clip, or be published on the Internet. Despite these new options, conventional books have advantages: they are inexpensive and portable, and do not need a power source to run them.

9–11 The cascading pages of this sculptural book emulate the flurry of wings when birds take flight. The shapes and shadows create a spiritual, uplifting feeling. Mary-Lise Beausire, (Switzerland), *L'envol III,* 1994. Handmade paper made from straw, 6 3/4 x 15 3/4 x 17 3/4" (17 x 40 x 45 cm).

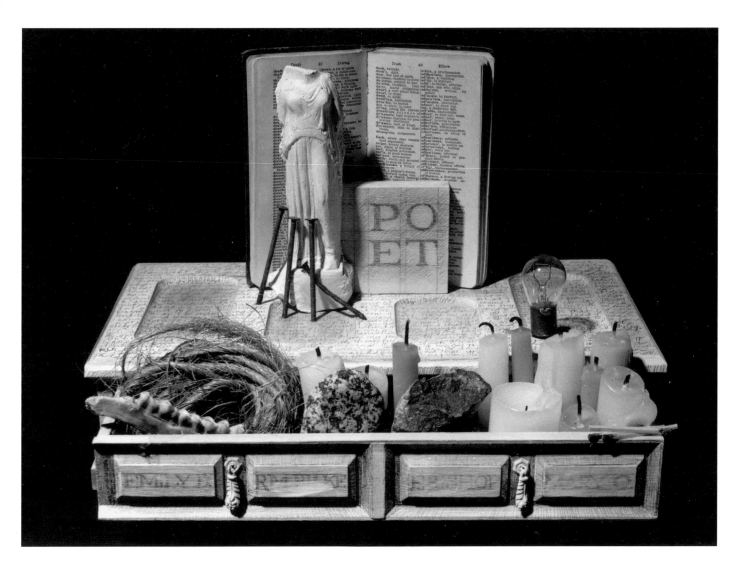

BOOKS AS SCULPTURE

Sculptural books are artists' books that are *unique*, or *one-off* (meaning that only one has been made). Sometimes called *bookworks*, they use the book form as the starting point for sculpture. These books rarely have much type, or look anything like traditional books. Their "stories" are told in their form. The artists must be clear about their message and specifically include it in the book. Sculptural books are not generally touched or picked up and read; rather, they are viewed or taken in as a whole at one time.

9–12 This mixed-media assemblage, exhibited as sculpture, serves as a dictionary of techniques for writing poetry. The light bulb represents insight; the stones, nature; the sculpture, classical literature and the Muses. Sas Colby (United States), *The Poet's Tool Box,* 1994. Mixed media assemblage with found objects, painted wooden box, acrylic, and pencil, 9 x 12 x 9 1/2" (22.7 x 30.5 x 24.1 cm).

FINE-PRESS BOOKS

Fine-press books are type-based works of art: their function is to beautify the literary text, and their illustrations are to amplify this text. Artistry and the consciousness of the book as a well-crafted object are also considered in fine-press books. The size of the type and the amount of white space are carefully balanced with the size of the page. The typeface and the style of illustration are chosen to suit the subject matter. These books are intended to be picked up and read from the first page to the last, allowing the reader to interact with them. Though they may have various formats and bindings, they are easily recognizable as books.

Fine-press books are printed in editions; that is, multiple identical copies are made, often by letterpress. Because there are many copies, many people can enjoy them. More affordable than one-off books, they are still more expensive than mass-market books. While some people believe that only one-off books can be considered artists' books, others consider fine-press books as artists' books if art was made a priority.

ALTERED BOOKS

Altered books are art pieces that use one or more existing commercially produced books as their starting point. The book or books are then cut, painted, pierced, piled up, burned, folded, or added to in some way to express the artist's message. Each is a unique work, or bookwork.

Books throughout history have been used to record and pass on information. Until paperbacks were commercially produced in 1935, books were relatively expensive and not affordable to the general public. Altered books often question the somewhat elitist position that books have had. Some of them comment on learning, literary themes, censorship, or politics.

9–13 The words in this fine-press concertina book are a quotation from John Muir, the American naturalist. For other examples of fine-press books see figures 3–8 and 9–9. Peter and Donna Thomas (United States), *Climb the Mountains*, 1995. Linoleum-cut print on handmade paper with pulp painting, 2 5/8 x 2 x 3/8" (6.8 x 5 x 1 cm), when closed.

9–14 What do you
see when you look at
this image? What is
the mysterious object
that appears to be
suspended in mid-
air? You are looking
at a page in a book;
on that page is a
photograph of trees
by the river in Paris.
The "floating" object
is the spot where the
artist sanded through
several layers of
pages, leaving what
looks like an elongat-
ed knot-hole in the
middle of the picture.
Douglas Beube
(United States), *Paris,
1994.* From the
Hypertexts series.
Altered book and
pictures, 7 1/2 x 5
1/2" (19 x 14 cm).

9–15 This book is an altered copy of *The Odyssey* (the story of Odysseus' travels), and is meant to indicate his wife's side of the story. The dried roses and thorns represent Penelope (Odysseus' wife) and her pain. She is symbolically bound to her husband by the copper wire. Joan Killion (United States), *Penelope's Version*, 1993. Dried roses bound with copper wire to a copy of *The Odyssey* in Greek; copper tacks nail the book closed amidst the thorns, 8 x 4 1/2 x 2" (20.3 x 11.4 x 5 cm).

9–16 Cathedrals are a favorite place to visit for this artist, who admires church architecture and its sense of tranquility. Dave Meder (Western Australia), *Cathedral,* 1995. An old paperback cut to shape using a craft knife, 7 7/8 x 11 x 5 1/2" (20 x 28 x 14 cm). Photo: Jean G. Kropper.

9–17 Parts of each page of this encyclopedia on science and technology were ripped out and reinserted into the book. The chambered nautilus, whose evolution is discussed on one of the pages, sits at the center of the work. Bird-like bits from the inside of sand dollars are glued across the pages. Margaret Whiting (United States), *Altered Book with Chambered Nautilus and Sand Dollar Pieces,* 1994. 11 x 18 x 4" (27.9 x 45.7 x 10.2 cm).

Children are usually taught to respect books and treat them gently. They are told, "Don't bend back the corners! Don't crack the spines!" The makers of altered books ignore those warnings. However, the point of altered books is not to destroy a book, but to use the book as an expressive art form to raise awareness of our assumptions about books and learning, and to examine their place in society.

It is best for children under twelve to make their own pamphlet books and then alter them. It is confusing to tell a child in one breath to treat books with respect, and then suggest in the next breath that they fold or rip the pages.

CREATIVE IDEAS

• Start with a discarded book and experiment with folding the pages individually or in groups of five. Fold the pages in on themselves, or fold the corners. How does this change the shape of the book? What is your reaction to touching a book like this?

• Shape the pages by cutting them with a craft knife (with a new blade) on a cutting mat. You will need to make many passes of the knife to cut through. Try a semicircle, a woman's profile, a triangle, or a house shape. Then open out the book and glue the front and back covers together to make a book in the round. What does the book look like?

• Find a discarded book. What is the book's subject? What is your response to it? What found objects would help communicate your message? Design an altered book around your answers to these questions.

10–1 This elaborate
scroll depicts history
and rituals from an
imagined world. Inga
Hunter (Australia),
Imperium Scroll,
1994. Collage on
canvas with a case;
etching, woodblock,
and linoblock prints;
paint and mixed
media, 5 1/8" x 3.3'
(13 cm x 1 m).

10–2 Unusual collage
materials and vibrant
colors bring these
handmade greeting
cards to life. Nancy
La Rose (United
States), 1995. Collage
of hand-marbled and
hand-combed papers,
ribbons, hand-dyed
silk, twigs, metal,
6 x 4 1/2" (15.2 x
11.4 cm).

DESIGN BEYOND THE ORDINARY

The techniques in this chapter offer ways to personalize your design and support the message of your books and cards. You can add texture with machine embroidery, dimension with pop-ups, or scent with essential oils, extending your work beyond just words or images on paper. This chapter also shows how skills you may already have—in painting, photography, or wood-carving—can be applied to books. Keep in mind how the use of one or more of these techniques could add to your work. Use them only if they are relevant; otherwise, they will detract from your message.

NOT JUST WORDS ON PAPER

COLLAGE

Collage gives cards and book covers a vitality and interest. The hoarders among us will be delighted to find a perfect use for recycling treasured bits and pieces. Collaged cards usually have stories connected to them—about a vacation, a reno-vation, a delicious meal, or a simple tour of the backyard. Cards or book covers can be decorated by arranging and gluing all sorts of different bits and pieces together into a pleasing arrangement. The different textures, type styles, and unusual materials are what make them distinctive. Collages are generally inex-pensive to make and are suitable for many occasions. You can add collage to blank cards you have made or bought; make sure you have envelopes to match.

10–3 Many items can be used in collage to decorate cards and books: handmade and unusual papers, iron-on fabric decorations, feathers, maps, old photographs, can-celed stamps, train tickets, and other items pictured here.

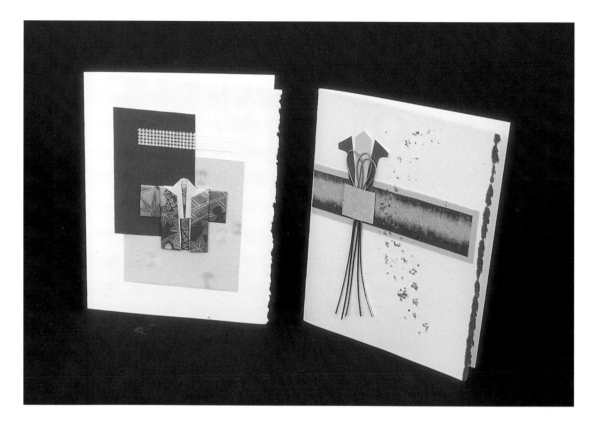

To make your own collage cards or book covers, first think about what materials you have on hand. In addition to items pictured in fig. 10–3, you could use old tourist brochures or postcards, leaves and flowers pressed flat, wood-veneer scraps, and upholstery fabric samples. For invitations to parties or celebrations where food will be served, you might use anise stars; dried watermelon seeds, wheat, or beans; magazine photos of food and drink; and old wine labels. (The natural materials are not appropriate for decorating book covers, however, because they are too fragile.)

For Christmas or Hanukkah cards, use glitter pens, fabric paint from a tube, spangles, scraps of colored papers, sections of bracken ferns that look like Christmas trees, scraps of gift wrap, tinsel, lace, braids, and images from old cards. You might spray-paint any of these items in gold or silver.

For wedding invitations and thank-you cards, try lace, pressed flowers, metal and plastic charms, papers in muted colors, soft-looking ripped paper edges, metallic inks, ribbon closures, or, if possible, leftover scraps of fabric from handmade bride or bridesmaid dresses.

PHOTOGRAPHS

Photographs can also be used in inventive ways. You can take images from books, magazines, newspapers, or video; computer-generate them; or download them from the Internet. You can take your own photographs and develop them; and then write a story or explanation, and design a book to hold them.

Try painting photographic chemicals on handmade paper and printing your images on the paper. The paper must be well sized to hold up in water (see page 24). Enlarge, reduce, and collage your photographs with other materials; or crop them to communicate your message. Photographs can have a silent emotional poignancy that words may not. Whatever photographic technique you try, always respect another photographer's copyright, and check whether you are allowed to use a photograph before going ahead with a project.

10–5 In creating this one-of-a-kind book, the artist brushed liquid photo emulsion onto Arches cold-press watercolor paper. This allowed her to print her own photographs from a trip to West Africa. Martha Fuller (United States), *West African Traces*, 1988. Bound in fabric from a local market, decorated with tassels, 15 1/2 x 12" (39.4 x 30.5 cm).

10–6 This book makes elaborate use of textures, manipulates photographic images, and pushes the capabilities of two-color offset printing to its full extent. Keith A. Smith (United States), *Book 89, Patterned Apart* (edition of 50), 1982. Arches cover paper, Curtis rag, offset-printed in blue and orange, watercolored prior to hand-binding in quarter leather, photos by the artist, 11 1/4 x 8 3/4 x 3/4" (28.6 x 21.6 x 2 cm), when closed. Produced by Space Heater Multiples.

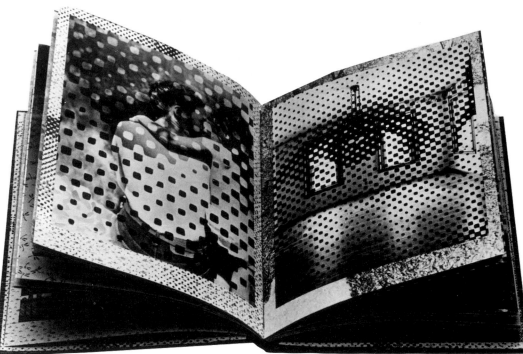

MACHINE EMBROIDERY ON PAPER

This simple, distinctive stationery makes use of the sewing machine. To use machine embroidery for an image or an abstract design for a book cover or a card, first sew on a thin piece of paper or fabric. Then glue the sewn piece onto heavier paper. (Your sewing machine may not be able to handle heavier paper.) Create an eye-catching, glitzy look with variegated metallic thread.

MATERIALS
- text-weight paper, commercial or handmade
- sewing machine thread in a contrasting color

DIRECTIONS

Thread your machine and set the stitch length at its longest. (Short stitches will rip through the paper.) If your machine can make decorative stitches, try them to see which you like. For stationery or cards, you can use winding lines around the edges, make a straight border down one side, or stitch different colors side by side. If you want to be more adventurous, cut layers of sheer fabrics, such as organza, into shapes to create images or landscapes; sew over them to anchor them in place. Or, decorate by using cording held down with a zigzag stitch. Experiment: you will often make your best discoveries by doing so.

CREATIVE IDEA

Create a tear-off coupon for a free dinner date; or make your own "special offer" in a book or card, or at the end of a letter. Use the sewing machine to make perforations in the paper. Set the machine on a short stitch length, and unthread the machine and remove the bobbin. Instead of making stitches with thread, the needle will poke a neat series of holes, or perforations, allowing the recipient to tear out your special offer.

10–7 A rhythmic pattern is created on the cover of this book using machine embroidery. B. E. Kloppers (Netherlands), *Be Deficient in Words*, 1993. Industrial paper, 18 1/8 x 12 5/8 x 1/2" (46 x 32 x 1 cm).

10–8 An unexpected combination of machine embroidery and appliqué with glittery fabric gives these original cards a vibrant look.

Gabriella Verstraeten (Australia), 1994. Satin, silk, and Lurex fabrics, and hand-beading, 5 x 7" (12.7 x 17.8 cm).

10–9 A whimsical concertina book shows the layers of clothing worn by a music conductor. When the book is closed, each layer is partially revealed. The size of the piece allows a person to hold the closed book in front of their body like a costume. Five people standing side by side behind the opened book would each appear to be wearing one of the layers of clothing. Martha Carothers (United States), *The Conductor,* 1984. Blueprints, lamination, and die-cut foam core pages, 18 x 18 x 108" (45.7 x 45.7 x 274.3 cm).

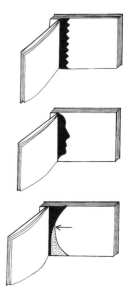

Shaped guards in hardcover albums

NOT JUST STRAIGHT EDGES

 ## SHAPED PAGES

A few shaped pages may be added to a rectangular book to produce a delightful surprise for the person looking through it. These differently shaped pages visually punctuate a book by dividing it into subject areas or chapters. They add interest and ensure that your hand-bound books will stand out from the commercially made crowd. Older dictionaries and address books often have shaped pages so that the reader can flip quickly to a particular listing.

Chapter 7 explained the use of guards in a scrapbook or photo album. These narrow strips are added to the spine to balance out the thickness of the photos and mementos glued into it. To make guards decorative as well as functional, try designing them as intriguing shapes that extend a bit into the page.

- For a diary, make a page in the shape of the writer's silhouette; for a recipe book, the shape of a piece of fruit; for a scrapbook, the shape of the border of a country you have visited.
- Create, as an art piece, a landscape of mountains, waves, or banks of clouds, using sequential pages of ripped tracing paper, which is translucent. You could also use opaque handmade or commercial papers.

10–10 Die-cut shaped pages in four shades of blue express the flow of a nearby river in this change-of-address announcement card. Didier Boursin (France), *The River Seine,* 1994. Commercial papers, 5 1/2 x 11" (14 x 28 cm).

 ## SHAPED BOOKS

Commercially made books are almost always rectangular; they fit on standard bookshelves in any bookstore. Shaped books are rarely made commercially: their production costs are high, and their display in bookstores becomes problematic.

However, hand-bound books are another matter. They do not have to fit on a particular shelf or look like other books, unless you want them to. You do not have to consider production costs as your priority. You can make your books in any shape or size—whatever suits you, the subject matter, and the users. How about a butterfly- or dragonfly-shaped book for poems? A book shaped like a bus, train, tractor, hexagon, pineapple, or heart? A book does not have to be a serious thing unless you want it to be.

10–11 Handmade books do not have to be rectangular. How about a fish-shaped book to record the details of your catch? A castle-shaped book for ghost stories? Made by the author.

10–12 This panoramic concertina book tells the story of the transformation of the land from wild landscape (left) to plowed field to urban cityscape with graffiti. Shaped pages, with panels of embedded text and images, make an intriguing design. Amanda Degener and Barbara A. Schubring (United States), *Land(scaped)* (edition of 80), 1994. Handmade paper, offset-printed photographs, 11 1/2 x 6 x 2" (29.2 x 15.2 x 5.1 cm), when closed. Photo: Barbara A. Schubring.

Make several sketches; then try to assess them objectively. What technique will you use to bind your book? Japanese stab-bound books are sewn on the left or on the top. Would this fit into your design? How will the book be used? Do not design a beautiful book that does not function well for its purpose. If you want to create a book as an art piece, that is fine; but if it is to be functional, keep its purpose in mind.

 ## SHAPED CARDS

Shaped cards stand out from the crowd. How about heart-shaped cards for Valentine's Day? A card in the shape of a birthday cake or a Christmas tree? A "we have moved" card in the shape of the new house? Or an invitation to a dinner celebration in the shape of a wine bottle? Just remember to leave an edge for the card's fold.

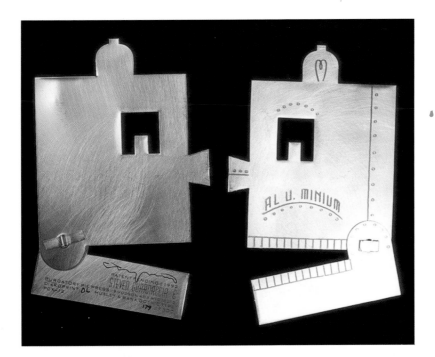

10–13 The artists wanted to showcase this press' capability for printing on metal, working with die cuts, and incorporating movable parts. This won an American Institute of Graphic Arts award. Esther K. Smith and Dikko Faust, with illustrations by Steven Guarnaccia (United States), *AL*U*MINIUM,* 1992. Letterpress printed and die-cut on aluminium, 6 x 4" (15.2 x 10.2 cm). Purgatory Pie Press, New York.

BEYOND TWO DIMENSIONS

POP-UPS

Pop-ups add another dimension to messages in books or cards; they literally stand out. Many of us fondly remember playing with the pop-up books we had as children, opening and closing those pages over and over. As adults, we can figure out how they work by tracing their cuts and folds when they are laid flat. There are many ways to build pop-ups, some quite complicated.

Pop-up photo cards are a simple, delightful way to send a personal three-dimensional message. They could remind someone close to you of a time you shared. You could show your news in a photograph of a birthday party, graduation, new house, wedding, or the flowers blossoming in your backyard.

MATERIALS
- metal ruler
- envelopes
- 80–100 lb (60–300 gsm) colored paper or drawing paper, 22 x 30" (55 x 75 cm), 1 sheet
- pencil
- triangle
- craft knife with a new blade
- cutting mat
- photograph
- newspaper
- glue stick or PVA glue and stencil brush
- bone folder
- nonstick paper

10–14 The Roman alphabet is based on letterforms chiseled in stone. Echoing this three-dimensional origin, the artist has designed pop-up letterforms that accent negative space and break through the edges of each page. Scott L. McCarney (United States), *Alphabook 1* (four volumes), 1981. Photos and pop-out letterforms, hand-cut and folded, 6 1/2 x 4 3/4" (16.5 x 12.1 cm).

10–15 Personalized pop-up cards made with photographs of family and friends can give the receiver a delightful surprise —and they are easy to make. Made by the author.

DIRECTIONS

1   Measure the size of the envelope you plan to use, and write down the height and width. Subtract at least 3/8" (10 mm) from each dimension; this will allow for the finished, folded card to fit easily into the envelope. Multiply either the height or the width by 2 (keep the second dimension the same) to get the size of the unfolded card. Using the triangle, metal ruler, craft knife, and cutting mat, mark with a pencil and then cut your selected paper to this size, keeping the grain parallel to the fold. Measure the halfway point, score the fold, and crease the card.

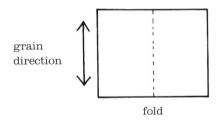

grain direction

fold

2   Measure and mark two slits about 1 1/4–2" (31–50 mm) long. Cut these carefully with the craft knife. Score the folds as shown, and bend the paper toward the inside of the card. This forms the base for your pop-up.

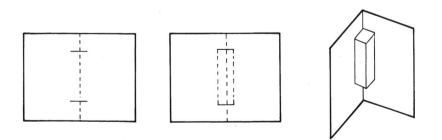

3 Choose the photo you want to use. Check that it will fit inside when the card is closed. Decide whether the card will be vertical or horizontal. Mask off the side of the pop-up section that will hold the photograph in place, and apply glue. Place the photograph in position. Cover it with clean scrap paper, and burnish it firmly with a bone folder so that it adheres. Throw away the scrap paper.

4 If you do not want the cutout fold to show from the outside, you can back the pop-up with a second card. To do this, cut a second blank card 1/8" (3 mm) larger than the first. Score and fold this second card in half, as before. Place the pop-up card flat (inside facing down) on a clean scrap of paper. Apply glue or glue stick to the outside, avoiding the pop-up section. Replace the used scrap paper with clean scrap paper. Put the pop-up card down again, glue side up. Place the blank card squarely on top, cover with nonstick paper, and burnish with a bone folder so that the cards adhere. Fold them together and trim the uneven edges. If you've used PVA glue, wrap the completed card in clean nonstick paper and then absorbent paper, and put it under a weight to dry. Cards glued with a glue stick do not need to be pressed.

5 You can handwrite a message on the card, use rub-down transfer lettering, or type and print out a message on a word processor to cut out and glue in place.

EMBOSSING

Embossing is creating a raised image, pattern, or initial in paper. By use of the tip of a bone folder or other *burnishing* tool, *embossments* are made by gradually stretching a heavy-weight paper into a metal or plastic template of letters or symbols. You can create a master stencil of your own design by cutting into a thick layer of smooth cardboard. Look at fig. 10–17. Notice that the embossing is being done on the back side of the paper, with the letters backwards; the letters will be right-reading when the paper is flipped over to the front. *Debossing* is creating a lowered image, pattern, or initial. The procedure is the same as embossing, but is done on the front side of the paper, using the front side of the stencil. Use a soft, thick paper so that it can be stretched over the design without ripping. Experiment on a corner of the paper you have chosen to test its suitability.

Embossing or debossing may be used as an elegant yet subtle decoration on the cover of a book or card, or on an inside page of a book. Embossings and debossings do not wear as well as a flat cover, which makes them impractical for a book that gets a lot of use. Printmakers emboss paper using uninked linoleum plates, woodcuts, or deeply etched metal plates. Slightly damp paper is placed on top of the plate, which is then run through the press as usual. (See fig. 10–18.)

10–16 The copper cover of this altered French-German dictionary has been embossed with randomly selected words. The piece is about the importance of the written word in our culture and the issue of censorship. Mary Ellen Long (United States), *Dictionnaire*, 1993. Copper covers, closed with polymer, 6 x 4 1/4 x 1 3/4" (15.2 x 10.8 x 4.4 cm).

10–17 With a burnisher or any round-tipped tool, you can slowly stretch paper over a template to create an embossed title, message, or initial. Photo: E. Lancaster.

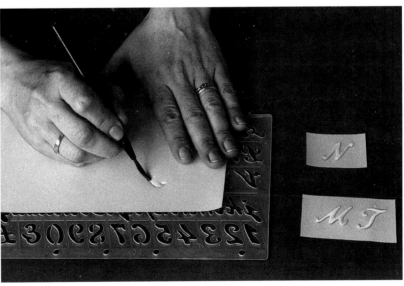

10–18 This embossed image was deeply carved into a linoleum block and pressed into the artist's handmade paper using an intaglio press. The force of the press pushed the paper into the grooves in the linoleum. Evalyn Prouty Hickman (United States), *Pima Basket Card* (Southwest series), 1995. Linoleum block print, handmade paper (cotton linter), 6 x 5 1/2" (15.2 x 14 cm).

WINDOWS

Windows are shaped holes cut into one or more pages, with a different-colored page, an image, or a patterned paper showing through the hole. A diamond-shaped window on one page could reveal a piece of marbling or gift wrap on the page behind it. An oval-shaped window could frame a small photo, piece of embroidery, or a pressed flower. Windows, like shaped pages, can be a way to punctuate a book, dividing it into chapters or sections. They are delightful surprises to the reader, and make your book unique.

You can cut the window in the shape of an image, such as a flower, a basketball, initials, the sun and moon, hearts, a tennis racket, leaves, an airplane, or a birthday cake. Come up with your own ideas. If the shapes are large or intricate, leave connecting strips between them for support, just as on a stencil.

MATERIALS
- pencil
- drawing paper
- craft knife with a new blade
- cutting mat
- blank card, cover paper for a book, or sequential pages of a book (bound or unbound)
- carbon paper or paper clips

10–19 Literally made from nature, this card features wildflowers from the Australian bush pressed between layers of contact plastic and mounted in windows cut in handmade paper. Meagan Gardiner (Western Australia), *Cards with a View* (a series), 1995. Handmade paper, plastic, 4 x 6" (10 x 15 cm).

10–20 Intricate designs cut into covers of these slender books are highlighted by contrasting paper underneath. Daphne Dobbyn (Australia), *Snowflakes* and *Flower*, 1994. Various commercial papers, left: 8 3/4 x 6 3/8 x 1/4" (22 x 16 x .7 cm), right: 8 7/8 x 6 3/8 x 1/2" (22.5 x 16 x 1.2 cm). Photo: E. Lancaster.

10–21 Students get creative with shaped windows, backing them with colored papers, in the author's workshop in Western Australia. Various sizes. Photo: Jean G. Kropper.

DIRECTIONS

1   After sketching ideas, draw the shape of the window to size in pencil on a piece of paper. Decide where the window will be placed on the card, book cover, or book page; it could be in one corner, or centered at the top or bottom. Keep the cuts 1/2" (12 mm) from the edges. (Cuts closer to the edge could rip as the page is handled.)

2   Use carbon paper to transfer the window's outline from your drawing onto the paper, or paper-clip the drawing in place and use it as a template during cutting. Open cards out flat before cutting. If the window is for the text page of a book, work with pages that are not yet bound. If you make a mistake, you can discard the page and start again. If the book is already bound, slide the cutting mat into the book, under the page to be cut.

3   Before cutting, take a few deep breaths. Cutting windows is delicate work and requires concentration. Practice cutting on scrap paper first. Then cut out the shapes in your window on your marked lines, one by one. Pause or lift your knife along the way, as needed.

UNUSUAL CLOSURES

Unusual closures date back to medieval times, when wooden covers and metal clasps were needed to hold humidity-sensitive parchment pages flat in a book. Without clasps, parchment could twist and buckle, distorting the books. In the 1200s, when paper began to replace parchment, clasps were no longer functional but were kept as a decorative device. Though clasps and ties are now virtually nonexistent on commercially published books, they are still used occasionally on diaries and hand-bound books as a decorative feature.

Many items can be used as closures for books: a tiny padlock (on a diary), a leather thong (on a sketchbook for landscapes), frogging (for a Chinese folktale), Velcro (for a poem about sneakers), a clothespin, hooks and eyes, a string wrapped around a button, or an elasticized tie with a charm on it. What closures might you try? What kind of book would be suitable for your subject matter? The closure should relate to the subject matter of your book: unusual closures add a distinctive touch but should not detract from what you have to say.

10–22 Delicate clasps and corner pieces were made by lost wax casting, then gilded. Multiple-section book with a lily-of-the-valley motif. Richard Minsky (United States), *Château Guest Book,* 1994. Calfskin binding, inlaid panel of lacquered acrylic and gold leaf, 8 3/4 x 6 3/8 x 1" (22.2 x 16 x 2.5 cm).

10–23 A folding hard case covered with parchment paper is fastened by a silk cord arranged in an elegant spiral. Inside are four softcover books containing pages taken at random from an old encyclopedia. Susan Rotolo (United States), *Cognitio Codex,* 1993. Paper, silk cord, 4 1/2 x 4 x 1 1/4" (11.4 x 10.2 x 3.2 cm).

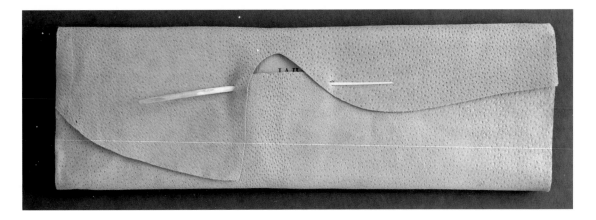

10–24 A wraparound leather cover is held closed with a tempered quill. Inside, 12 unbound pages portray aspects of the El Molino del Manzano Papermill in Buenos Aires, Argentina, where it was made. Anne Vilsbøll (Denmark) and Sophie Dawson (England), *La Illusion Verde*, 1993. Handmade paper, leather, quill, 6 x 17 3/4 x 1/2" (15.3 x 45 x 1 cm).

🌲 ADDING SCENT

Scents can evoke all sorts of occasions and memories. A particular scent may cause one person to remember a romantic evening, while the same scent may cause another person to recall a day of adventure. The person who receives your scented card may be treated to his or her own memories associated with the scent.

Choose the card or book to which you will add scent. Then choose what you want to use for scent: cloves, cinnamon, curry, eucalyptus, pine, potpourri, lavender, perfume, or essential oils. Use a box, plastic container, or cookie tin that is large enough to hold your card or book. The container must have a tight-sealing lid.

Place the card or book in the container. If you use spices, just sprinkle them into the container. Do not put oils or perfume on the card or book itself: they will leave a stain. Instead, put the liquid on an absorbent piece of paper inside the container with the card or book. Seal the container and leave it for a few weeks, allowing the scent to permeate the paper.

10–25 Ten removable cards with dessert recipes, each with its own scratch-and-sniff illustration, fill the pockets of this imaginative miniature concertina. A pop-up fruit bowl adorns the title page. Pat Baldwin (United States), *Fruity Jubilee* (edition of 50), 1995. Printed on Fabriano and handmade banana-fiber paper in Parisian type using a color printer, cloth over cover boards, 2 3/4 x 2 3/8" (7 x 6 cm). Printed at Pequeño Press, bound at Waterleaf Mill and Bindery.

10–26 Add scent to cards, stationery, or books by sealing them in a container with perfume, scented oils, cinnamon sticks, or potpourri.

10–28 Reviving historic methods of bookbinding, the artist made his own paper, leather, thread, and wooden covers by hand. A Celtic pattern is carved on the covers and fore edge, adding an original touch to this handsome pair of books. Jim Croft Traditional Hand Craft Study Group (United States), *Late Medieval Style Blank Book,* 1995. Wood, handmade flax and hemp paper pages, bound with hand-spun homegrown flax thread, alum-tawed leather and bronze clasps, 5 1/2 x 4 x 2" (14 x 10.2 x 5.1 cm).

10–27 One of the earliest known dos-à-dos bindings, this unusual collection of poetry features gilt and gauffered edges in a floral pattern with red-and-green paint. (Germany) *Strozzi poetae,* 1582. Calfskin-over-pasteboard cover, 6 1/2 x 4 1/2 x 2 1/4" (16.5 x 11.5 x 5.5 cm). The Pierpont Morgan Library, New York. PML 51588.

GOFFERED AND SCULPTED EDGES

Goffered (or *gauffered*) edges are traditionally made by a laborious technique that involves gilding a book's edges and using a hot metal tool to hammer in designs. The Italians adopted this distinctive technique from the East; then the Spanish picked it up and began gilding and goffering the edges of Christian books as early as 1400. The practice spread, and by the early 1500s, gilding and goffering were used in the courts of northern Europe.

Few people today have the skill or the time to make goffered edges in the traditional way. However, you can experiment with cutting, carving, or hammering decorative leather or jeweler's punches (circular or patterned) against a book's fore edge, head, or tail. For a wide enough surface to carve, the book must contain at least 100 pages. Experiment on several old paperbacks until your work becomes consistent and you feel pleased with the results. Otherwise, you could go through all the work of binding your own book only to ruin it at the end.

Jim Croft, an Indiana book artist who is one of the few people worldwide using this technique today, advises: "Fore-edge carving is not much more difficult than carving wood. Clamp the book tightly, then use wood-carving tools, such as gouges and chisels, scrapers and sandpaper to carve it, just as you would a dense piece of wood. After carving, you can rub beeswax onto the fore edge with a cloth. Buff with a second cloth afterwards."

Place a piece of cardboard or plywood on both covers of the book to protect them in the vise, and be careful to keep the book clean. Use sharp chisels to make precise cuts. You might also try saws. Whatever cutting tool you choose, use it safely. This technique isn't for the fainthearted; but, like fore-edge painting, it sets your books apart.

PAINTED FORE EDGES

Usually, the titles on books made in the Middle Ages were painted on one edge. This was for easy identification because the books were stored in piles in chests. Later, in the Renaissance, books were stored on tables or sloping shelves, so titles were put on the books' front covers. By the late 1600s, some books were displayed upright on shelves. In Spain and England, the fore edges faced outward. This encouraged decoration with goffering or painted titles, often color-coded by subject or author. This practice continued until the late 1600s, when books began to be stored with the spines outward, and the titles on the spine.

A fore edge can be painted either *edge on*, when the book is closed; or with the pages *flexed*, when the book is open. When the fore edge is painted while the pages are flexed, the painting can't be seen when the book is closed. This is called *disappearing fore-edge painting*, which provides a dramatic surprise for the reader.

flexed fore edge

10–29 A hand-painted top edge decorates this re-creation of a diary that belonged to a seventeenth century Polish nobleman. Joan Iversen Goswell (United States), *Vienna 1683*, 1984–85. Hand written and illustrated on handmade paper from the Barcham Green Mill, endsheets from Fabriano mill; gouache, watercolor, raised gold, silk endbands, 7 x 10 x 3/4" (17.8 x 25.4 x 1.9 cm).

10–30 A portrait of Charles II graces the fore edge of this multisection book from seventeenth-century England. *Dieu et mon droit*, c. 1660. Binding in leather with mosaic and gold-tooled decoration; fore edge: 15.4 x 10 x 3 1/4" (39 x 25 x 8.3 cm). By permission of the Houghton Library, Harvard University.

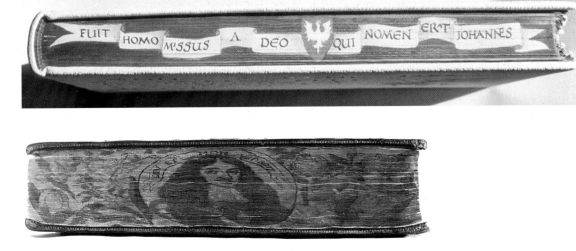

Recalling the decorative quality of earlier fore-edge painting, Edwards of Halifax and London (a publisher, binder, and bookseller) revived and popularized fore-edge painting in the early 1800s. However, instead of titles, the book owner's portrait or country estate was painted on the disappearing fore edge.

Although fore edges are rarely painted now, the technique is quite simple. You can apply watercolor or gouache paint with a fine brush. Thin the paint with water. If the paint is too thick, it will make the pages stick together. If the paint is too watery and it is applied heavily, the edges of the pages will warp.

Sketch the image to size. Begin by experimenting on several old paperbacks until your work becomes consistent and you feel pleased with the results. If you make a mistake, let the paint dry, and then clamp the book between two boards in a vise. Sand the edge until the paint is gone. Start again. You will need patience and a steady hand. Though this elaborate form of decoration may be beyond the skill level of many bookbinders, it is a wonderful finishing touch that can decidedly separate a handmade book from the commercially made crowd.

REFERENCE

GLOSSARY

acid-free paper Paper that is chemically neutral on the pH scale and can last as long as 300 years. This means that it will not break down chemically or change over time. Newspaper is not acid-free and will become brittle and yellow with age.

accordion book *See* concertina book.

album binding A stab binding (used for hardcover scrapbooks and photo albums) that is simplified so that the binding can be undone, pages can be added or removed, and the book can be rebound.

archival Referring to lasting indefinitely in top condition without any chemical deterioration.

archivite A dense cardboard made for bookbinding. *See* boards.

artist's book A book made by an artist, a book that is a piece of art in itself, or a book that takes artistic issues (binding, size, format, materials used) into consideration to communicate the artist's message; may be unique or editioned.

barrier cream A heavy hand cream for people who work with their hands; used to prevent chapping or to reduce the absorption of chemicals through the skin.

bleed To fan out in a thick, spidery line, as when ink from a pen is absorbed into unsized paper. (Paper does not bleed when it is sized appropriately.) *See* sizing.

boards The generic term for the cardboard, greyboard, archivite, or other material used for the covers of a book.

bone folder A smooth tool made of bone that looks like a rounded tongue depressor with one pointed end. It is used to score papers, crease folds, shape embossings, and burnish and smooth papers.

bookwork A unique (or one-off) artwork, often sculptural, based on the book as a concept. It may or may not have text, images, pages, or covers.

Cover boards like these from twelfth-century Europe were actual wooden boards covered with leather. Multiple sections sewn onto split leather thongs are attached to the cover boards through holes drilled near the spine. *Sacramentary for the Cathedral of Urgel*, Catalonia, c. 1150. Parchment pages, 11 3/4 x 8 3/4 x 2 3/8" (29.8 x 22.2 x 6 cm). Pierpont Morgan Library. Photo: PML M 922

burnishing The act of rubbing or applying pressure, with a bone folder or other tool, to papers or boards that have been glued or pasted together. This expels air bubbles and ensures an even join.

case-bound book A book whose case, or cover, is made separately from the book and added later.

codex A manuscript made up of sheets or folios bound down one side (at the spine) and protected by covers. This traditional format is used for most commercially made Western books.

colophon A paragraph at the end of an editioned book stating the details of who wrote, printed, and bound the book; the number of books in the edition; the printing process; the place it was made; and the date.

complex binding Two or more binding techniques combined in one book.

concertina book A book whose binding is formed by accordion, or zigzag, folds in a long strip of paper. The folds create the pages of the book. Also known as an accordion or leporello book.

Coptic book A book bound with a Coptic binding; covers and sections are bound together at the same time with no other support. The binding is exposed.

cover paper or **cover stock** Paper that is 80–100 lb (170–260 gsm), the correct weight for a book cover or a card.

crossed-ribbon binding A recently invented binding technique for a stab-bound book or album; ribbon is used in place of thread and crisscrosses the spine.

cutting mat or **cutting board** Special mats used as a cutting surface, designed not to dull knife blades. Some vinyl cutting mats are self-sealing.

deboss To lower the surface of paper in the shape of a design in relief. *See* emboss.

disappearing fore-edge painting A painting done on the fore edge of a book while its pages are flexed. When the book is closed (and the pages are not flexed), the painting is not visible.

dos-à-dos French for "back to back," a traditional book format in which two related books are bound together with a common back cover.

dummy A mock-up, or a pretend book, used as a model of the finished book, to aid in its planning and design.

edition Refers collectively to identical copies of a book that were printed at the same time.

editioning The process of making multiple, identical copies of a book.

emboss To raise the surface of paper in the shape of a design in relief.

embossment The raised-surface product of embossing; also, the process of embossing.

endpaper The paper on the inside of the front and back covers of a book; in some bindings, the endpaper continues across the crease and becomes the first free leaf between the covers and the text. Endpapers are often decorated but are not given page numbers.

film positive Transparent film having photographically reproduced type or images that are right-reading, not reversed.

flyleaf, or **flysheet** The first or second free page inside a book cover (depending on the type of binding used), before the text.

folio, or **fold** A single sheet of paper that has been folded once. This becomes two leaves, or four pages or sides.

fore edge The edge of the book that opens, opposite the spine. In a codex or Western format book, it is the right edge.

format A book's design: its size, style, page layout, typography, and binding.

French-door format A book or card format that hinges from both the right and left sides, like French doors.

gate fold format See French-door format.

goffer (or **gauffer**) An old technique of gilding and hammering designs into a book's edges.

grain The cellulose fibers in paper that are aligned parallel to one another within the sheet as paper is made. Folds made parallel to the grain will be straighter and more durable than those made across the fibers.

grain direction The orientation of the fibers within a sheet of paper.

greyboard See boards.

gutter The white space on a page between the type and the spine (also known as the inside margin).

hard edge An edge that is cut perfectly clean with a sharp knife.

head The top horizontal edge of a book when it is upright; the edge opposite the tail and perpendicular to both the spine and fore edge.

hinge The point where a cover bends to open.

Japanese stab-bound book A book that is bound by sewing through holes punched or stabbed through both the cover and text pages along the spine edge.

leading The vertical space between lines of type.

leaf A sheet of paper in its entirety; it includes both sides, or pages.

leather punch A tool that is struck with a hammer and used to punch holes in covers or in a stack of papers.

leporello book See concertina book.

letterpress A printing technique that uses raised metal type and images that are inked and pressed against a sheet of paper.

letterspacing The relative distance between characters within a line of type.

methyl cellulose A vegetable-based sizing or adhesive commonly sold by bookbinding suppliers (acid free) and in hardware stores as wallpaper paste (not acid-free).

miter To taper or cut the corners at an angle before joining. Specifically, to taper the top and bottom of the tabs of the sections of a concertina before joining them together. This prevents the tabs from showing on the head and tail of the completed book.

mock-up See dummy.

mountain fold A fold that points upward, like a mountain.

needles Two kinds are used for binding: sharply pointed straw or embroidery needles (also for piercing holes), and blunt-tipped bookbinding or tapestry needles.

nip To press glued or pasted sheets of paper (in a press) and release immediately.

offset printing A lithographic technique that uses metal or paper photo-mechanical plates to transfer images onto a rubber blanket covering a roller drum (offsetting them) and then onto the paper.

one-off, or **unique** A term that means that only one copy of a book was made.

open content A book's content that has not yet been determined at the time of binding. Examples of open-content books are scrapbooks, diaries, and photo albums.

page One side of a sheet of paper, or leaf, that has writing on it.

pamphlet A one-section softcover book or booklet bound by sewing or stapling into the crease.

pamphlet stitch or **pamphlet binding** A simple binding technique used to connect a number of folios, or folded sheets of paper, in a soft cover. Pamphlets have only one section.

paste A reversible adhesive made from cooked wheat or rice flour and used for attaching paper to paper. Paste comes in both acid-free and nonacid-free forms.

pica A typography measurement that specifies distances such as column widths or gutters. There are six picas in one inch.

point A typography measurement commonly used to specify the type size. There are twelve points in one pica.

PVA (polyvinyl acetate), or **white glue** A flexible, fast-drying, non-reversible surface adhesive used on paper or cardboard, and available in both acid-free and nonacid-free forms.

right-reading Referring to type or images that can be read as usual, and are not upside down or backwards.

scriptorium A room where medieval monks or nuns copied manuscripts.

section, or **signature** (in printing) A unit of several folios, or folded sheets of paper, bound in a book.

sequencing The process of determining the order of a book's contents.

serif Typography term for the tail or line extending from the top or bottom of the main line or stroke of a letter. Letters without serifs are *sans serif*.

set content A book's content that is complete at the time of binding.

sewing station A hole pierced in a book for binding.

sizing A chemical added to paper; it increases strength and reduces the paper's absorbency. Sizing fills in the crevices between the paper's individual cellulose fibers, and prevents ink or paint from bleeding when applied to the paper. *See* bleed.

soft edge An irregular torn or deckle edge on handmade paper.

spine A book's back edge, where the pages are sewn or glued together. In a codex or typical Western book, it is the left side.

spring-loaded dividers An instrument for measuring or marking, used especially to measure a distance which will be matched elsewhere.

square In a hardcover book, the part of the cover that overhangs the text pages.

square knot or **reef knot** A common double knot for connecting two thread or rope ends; the knot tightens when stress is put on either side.

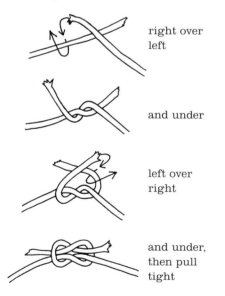

right over left

and under

left over right

and under, then pull tight

stab binding *See* Japanese stab-bound book.

star book or **star card** A book or card—made from folded, glued squares of paper—that has a star shape when open.

tail The lower horizontal edge of a book when held upright; the edge opposite the head and perpendicular to both the spine and fore edge.

tawed (or **alum-tawed**) Referring to the process of treating animal skin (usually goat skin or pigskin) with aluminum salts and other substances, and producing a soft white skin different from leather.

text pages, or **text block** The pages between the covers that contain the content of a book.

text paper Paper that is the correct weight, 20–24 lb (80–120 gsm), suitable for the text pages of a book.

treasure binding A book cover decorated with panels of ivory, tooled leather, gold, silver, or semiprecious and precious stones; produced mostly from 800 to 1200.

tunnel book A form of concertina book in which pages are mounted between two concertinas. The book is viewed through cutout shapes in the front pages, which expose parts of the pages behind.

typography The arrangement and appearance of printed matter.

valley fold A fold that points down, like a valley.

vellum A high-quality parchment made from a thin layer of calfskin that is rubbed with pumice and then treated. Sometimes the term refers to commercial papers that have similar properties to vellum: those that are off-white and sturdy, and have a waxy translucent look.

weaver's knot A knot for joining a new thread to an old one in the middle of a binding. (See illustration on page 109.)

weight The weight of paper is measured in grams per square meter. A text paper is 20–24 lb (80–20 gsm), and a cover stock is 80–100 lb (170–260 gsm). Paper chosen for a book must have the proper weight (or thickness) for the book's use and size.

Metric paper sizes are widely used in all Western cultures except for the United States. Commonly used sizes are as follows:

Sheet Size	Millimeters	Approx. Inches
A2	420 x 594	16 1/2 x 23 3/8
A3	297 x 420	11 3/4 x 16 1/2
A4	210 x 297	8 1/4 x 11 3/4
A5	148 x 210	5 7/8 x 8 1/4
A6	105 x 148	4 1/8 x 5 7/8
A7	74 x 105	2 7/8 x 4 1/8

Envelope Size	Millimeters	Approx. Inches
C2	458 x 648	18 x 25
C3	324 x 458	12 3/4 x 18
C4	229 x 334	9 x 12 1/2
C5	162 x 229	6 3/8 x 9
C6	114 x 162	4 1/2 x 6 3/8
C7	81 x 114	3 1/4 x 4 1/2

CONVERSION EQUIVALENTS

Linear Measure

1 meter = 39.37 inches, 3.2808 feet, 1.0936 yards

1 centimeter = 0.3937 inch

1 millimeter = 0.03937 inch

1 yard = 0.9144 meter

1 foot = 304.8 millimeters

1 inch = 2.54 centimeters, 25.4 millimeters

10 millimeters (mm) =1 centimeter (cm)

100 centimeters (cm) = 1 meter

Multiply	By	To Obtain
inches	2.54	centimeters
inches	25.4	millimeters
Divide	**By**	**To Obtain**
centimeters	2.54	inches
millimeters	25.4	inches

RESOURCES

NEWSLETTERS

Ampersand: Alliance for
Contemporary Book Arts
P.O. Box 24415
Los Angeles, CA 90024
(818) 906-9971

Book Arts Classified and Book Arts
Directory
Page Two, Inc.
2718 SW Kelly Street, Suite 222
Portland, OR 97201
(800) 821-6604

Bookways
1906 Miriam Avenue
Austin, TX 78722-1714
(512) 478-7414

Hand Papermaking
P.O. Box 582571
Minneapolis, MN 55458-2571

Journal of Artist's Books
Brad Freeman
324 Yale Avenue
New Haven, CT 06515

Umbrella Associates
P.O. Box 40100
Pasadena, CA 91114
(310) 399-1146
(News on artist's books)

U & lc (Upper and lower case)
P.O. Box 129
Plainview, NY 11803-0129
(Newsletter on typography)

TOOLS AND MATERIALS

The Bookbinder's Warehouse, Inc.
31 Division Street
Keyport, NJ 07735
(908) 264-0306
Fax: (908) 264-8266
e-mail: KarenC5071@aol.com

Bookmakers, Ltd.
6001 Sixty-Sixth Avenue, Suite 101
Riverdale, MD 20737
(301) 459-3384
Fax: (301) 459-7629

Colophon Book Arts Supply, Inc.
3046 Hogum Bay Road NE
Olympia, WA 98516
(206) 459-2940

The Harcourt Bindery
51 Melcher Street
Boston, MA 02210
(617) 542-5858
Fax: (617) 451-9058

Talas
568 Broadway
New York, NY 10012
(212) 736-7744

GROUPS

Each of these groups is national and
has a newsletter.

The Canadian Bookbinders and Book
Artists Guild
35 McCaul Street, Suite 220
Toronto, Ontario M5T 1V7
Canada

Friends of Dard Hunter
Wavell Cowan, Membership VP
Box 50, HCR 34
Montpelier, VT 05602
(802) 223-6362
Fax: (802) 223-3480
(Newsletter and annual conferences
for people interested in paper, its histo-
ry, and conservation; for bookbinders,
book artists, and hand-papermakers)

The Guild of Bookworkers
521 Fifth Avenue
New York, NY 10175
(suppliers list and newsletter)

CENTERS

Each offers workshops, exhibitions,
and information.

Ah Haa School for the Book
and Story Arts
P.O. Box 1590
Telluride, CO 81435
(303) 728-3886

Center for The Book
102 EPB, University of Iowa
Iowa City, IA 52240
(319) 335-0438

Center for Book and Paper Arts
Columbia College Chicago
218 South Wabash Avenue, 7th floor
Chicago, IL 60604
(312) 431-8612
Fax: (312) 986-8237

Center for Book Arts
626 Broadway, 5th floor
New York, NY 10012
(212) 460-9768

Dieu Donne Papermill
3 Crosby Street
New York, NY 10013
(212) 226-0573

Magnolia Editions
2527 Magnolia Street
Oakland, CA 94607
(510) 839-5268
Fax: (510) 893-8334

Minnesota Center for the Book Arts
24 North Third Street
Minneapolis, MN 55401
(612) 338-3634

NY Women's Studio Workshop
P.O. Box 489
Rosendale, NY 12472
(914) 658-9133

The Papertrail
1546 Chatelain Avenue
Ottawa, Ontario KIZ 8B5
Canada
(613) 728-4669

Pyramid Atlantic
6001 Sixty-sixth Avenue, #102
Riverdale, MD 20737
(301) 459-7154

University of Alabama
P.O. Box 870252
Tuscaloosa, AL 35487-0252
(205) 348-1525

PAPERS, PAPERMAKING SUPPLIES, AND WORKSHOPS

Carriage House Paper
79 Guernsey Street
Brooklyn, NY 11222
Tel/Fax: (718) 599-7857
(800) 669-8781

Lee S. McDonald, Inc.
P.O. Box 264
Charlestown, MA 02129
(617) 242-2505
Fax: (617) 242-8825

Rugg Road Paper
105 Charles Street
Boston, MA 02114
(617) 742-0002

Twinrocker
P.O. Box 413
Brookston, IN 47923
(800) 757-TWIN

BIBLIOGRAPHY

Abel, Michele. *The Art of Rubber Stamping: Easy as 1, 2, 3.* Wayzata, MN: Creative Press, Inc., 1991.

Burns, Stephanie. *Great Lies We Live By.* Crows Nest, Australia: Caminole Pty, Ltd., 1993.

Burns, Stephanie. *Artistry in Training.* Mona Vale, Australia: Woods Lane Press, 1996.

Chambers, Anne. *A Guide to Making Decorated Papers.* London: Andre Deutsch, Ltd., 1988.

Chatani, Masahiro, and Keiko Nakagawa. *Paper Magic: Pop-Up Paper Craft.* Tokyo: Ondorisha Publishers, Ltd., 1988.

Diehl, Edith. *Bookbinding: Its Background and Technique.* New York: Dover Publications, 1980.

Diringer, David. *The Book Before Printing: Ancient, Medival, and Oriental.* New York: Dover Publications, Inc., 1982.

Doty, Betty, and Rebecca Meredith. *Hey Look... I Made a Book!* Berkeley, CA: Ten Speed Press, 1992.

Drucker, Johanna. *The Century of Artist's Books.* New York: Granary Books, 1996.

Gaylord, Susan Kapuscinski. *Multicultural Books to Make and Share.* New York: Scholastic Professional Books, 1994.

Green, Jean Drysdale. *Arteffects.* New York: Watson-Guptill Publications, 1993.

Hiner, Mark. *Paper Engineering: For Pop-up Books and Cards.* Norfolk, England: Tarquin Publications, 1985.

———. *Up-Pops: Paper Engineering with Elastic Bands.* Norfolk, England: Tarquin Publications, 1991.

Ikegami, Kojiro. *Japanese Bookbinding.* New York: John Weatherill, 1990.

Jackson, Paul. *The Encyclopedia of Origami and Papercraft Techniques.* Philadelphia and London: Running Press Book Publishers, 1991.

———. *The Pop-Up Book.* New York: Henry Holt and Company, 1993.

Johnson, Pauline. *Creative Bookbinding.* New York: Dover Publications, 1990.

Kropper, Jean G. *Papermaking: From Recycling to Art.* Port Melbourne, Australia: Lothian Books, 1994.

LaPlantz, Shereen. *Cover to Cover.* New York: Sterling, 1995.

Leland, Nita, and Virginia Lee Williams. *Creative Collage Techniques.* Cincinnati, OH: North Light Books, 1994.

Lewis, Roy Harley. *Fine Bookbinding in the Twentieth Century.* New York: Arco Publishing, Inc., 1985.

Lloyd, Linda. *Classroom Magic Amazing Technology for Teachers and Home Schoolers.* Portland: Metamorphous Press, 1990.

McCarthy, Bernice. *The 4Mat System Teaching to Learning Styles with Right/Left Mode Techniques.* Barrington, IL: Excel, Inc., 1987.

McCarthy, Bernice. *About Learning.* Barrington, IL: Excel, Inc., 1996.

Premchand, Neeta. *Off the Deckle Edge: A Papermaking Journey Through India.* Bombay: The Ankur Project, 1995.

Rigaut, Henriette. *La Reliure Comme un Professionnel.* Paris: Editions Flerurus.

Rudin, Bo. *Making Paper: A Look into the History of an Ancient Craft.* Vallingby, Sweden: Rudins, 1990.

Ryst, Marie. *Carnets et Albums: Comment les Relier.* Paris: Bordas Dessain et Tolra, 1996.

Shannon, Faith. *Paper Pleasures.* Sydney, Australia: Angus and Robertson, 1987.

Simmons, Rosemary, and Katie Clemson. *The Complete Manual of Relief Printmaking.* Sydney, Australia: Collins Publishers Australia, 1988.

Smith, Gloria Zmolek. *Teaching Hand Papermaking: A Classroom Guide.* Cedar Rapids, IA: Zpaperpress, 1995.

Smith, Keith A. *Nonadhesive Binding: Books without Paste or Glue, Book 128.* 3rd ed. Rochester, NY: Keith A. Smith Books, (22 Cayuga Street, Rochester, NY 14620-2153), 1995.

———. *Nonadhesive Binding, 1, 2 & 3-Section Sewings, Book 169.* 3rd ed. Rochester, NY: Keith A. Smith Books, 1995.

———. *Nonadhesive Binding, Exposed Spine Sewings, Book 170.* Rochester, NY: Keith A. Smith Books, 1995.

———. *Structure of the Visual Book, Book 95.* 3rd ed. Rochester, NY: Keith A. Smith Books, 1995.

———. *Text in the Book Format, Book 120.* 2nd ed. Rochester, NY: Keith A. Smith Books, 1995.

Taylor, W. S., ed. *The Thames and Hudson Manual of Book Binding.* England: Thames and Hudson, 1992.

Typography: The Type Directors Club Annual. New York: Watson-Gulptill Publications, yearly publication.

Watts, Lynda. *Making Your Own Cards.* London: New Holland Publishers, Ltd., 1994.

Zeier, Franz. *Books, Boxes and Portfolios.* New York: Design Press, 1990.

INDEX